CARS

SELECTA

First published in England 1993 by
Wordsworth Editions Ltd
Cumberland House
Crib Street
Ware
Hertfordshire SG12 9ET

Copyright © 1992 Aldino Ltd
147 Cleveland Street, London W1P 5PH

ISBN 1 85326 994 8

Photographs by courtesy of TRH Pictures, London
Right: The McLaren F1 unveiled in Monte Carlo
in May 1992, powered by a V12 6.1-litre BMW
engine producing 408kW (550PS)

Set in 8½/9pt Monophoto Univers
Text conversion and pagination by
August Filmsetting, St Helens

Printed in Italy by Amadeus s.p.a.

Contents

Datsun's most successful muscle car,
4 *the 240Z*

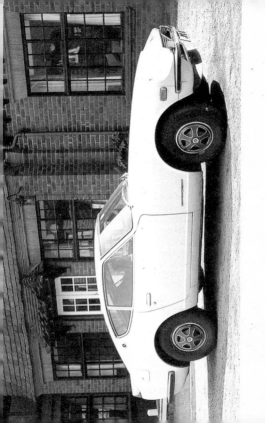

1992 Mercedes-Benz 300 SL, powered by a 24V 3-litre engine

8   A standard Porsche 911 of 1964

Introduction

It is not easy to define a sports car; originally, the guidelines suggested that it sacrificed comfort, convenience and even ease of driving in order to go faster and handle better than ordinary saloon cars of similar price. Today these parameters have to be tossed aside.

The most obvious sacrifice of convenience is to reduce the seating, to enable the production of a lighter, smaller and therefore faster car. The original concept of the 1930s utilised another weight-saving ploy, that of cutting off the car's roof and fitting a light canvas hood; but as design developed away from the separate chassis and into more efficient unitary construction, the convertible car might well be heavier than its equivalent with closed steel roof, which would also make the car stronger. In the 1980s a new generation of convertible saloons emerged, intended for those who enjoy open-air motoring and with no pretence of being 'sporting'.

To capture as wide a market as possible, the sports car has diversified. The highest performance cars have always been expensive, but in the 1950s a new breed of 'Grand Touring' (GT) car emerged, to combine sporting performance with great comfort and luxury. We cannot exclude these; to do so would eliminate some of the

The MGB typified the open sports cars continued today by the Mazda
10 *MX5 Miata and the Lotus Elan*

OUR MOTHER WOULDN'T LIKE IT.

finest sporting cars. They are high performers, whether they are two-seaters or more and they are the rich man's image-maker.

What we have omitted is the specialised sports-racing car. Although racing originally was for open two-seaters either on the track or the open road, changes in regulations were made in response to the rulebending by individuals and companies determined to win. These have triggered development but also resulted in the specialisation track racers.

The sports car has its origins in the pioneer days of motoring before World War I, when motoring was still expensive enough to be regarded as a rich man's hobby. Early motor races were run in the UK for roadgoing cars which had the bodywork stripped down to the bare minimum. However, meanwhile in America the Ford Model T meant that motoring was no longer exclusive. Some manufacturers were to offer models which went fast and handled better than the 'Tin Lizzie'; thus some of the first sports cars built in quantity, like the Mercer Race-about and the Stutz Bearcat, appeared in the USA.

The golden age of the sports car dawned in Europe after the end of World War I. The motorcar became more common, and drivers wanted to indulge their enthusiasm. The standard small saloon cars of those days were very

crude, and it was not difficult for a skilled engineer to improve both chassis and engine. Jaguar began by converting Austin Sevens, and MGs were rebodied Morris saloons.

At the same time, some engineers realised that they could do better still by starting with a clean sheet of paper: hence the multitude of small-scale production lines like AC, Aston Martin, Fraser-Nash and Lea-Francis in the UK; Amilcar, Delage, Hotchkiss and Salmson in France; Alfa Romeo in Italy, not to mention the work of the legendary engineer Bugatti, achieving sporting performance through light weight, attention to detail and an uncanny feeling for chassis design, when very little was understood about the reasons why cars handled as they did.

The 1930s saw more cheap sports cars, offering a wider choice and better quality. MG and Morgan were joined by Riley and Singer; at the other end of the sports car market, the large Delahaye made its mark. In America Auburn, Cord and Duesenberg produced their classics, while Mercedes and BMW continued to provide for an ever-eager market.

A great deal of this changed following World War II. In North America the 'big four' manufacturers had absorbed the classic names, but the

14 *A 1929 Bugatti, made following the 1926 and 1928 racing seasons*

British kept alive the tradition with the Jaguar XK 120, the Healey 100, the Triumph TR2 and the Austin Healey Sprite, which offered the motorist real excitement at affordable prices. Italy followed with the emergence of Ferrari, along with its great rival, Maserati.

The 1960s were another era of change. Some of the last of the traditional sports car names were almost allowed to die or ended as mere high-performance versions of standard saloons. Yet engineers like Colin Chapman, surely the nearest postwar equivalent to Bugatti in the way he advanced the understanding of chassis and suspension design, gained real stature with the Elite and Elan, and moved onto more modern cars in the GT mould. Lamborghini, de Tomaso and Iso joined the longer-established companies in the Italian GT industry, while in Germany Porsche became a force to be reckoned with as the 911 made a name for itself.

In America a small-volume specialist could never gain so much as a toehold in a massive market, yet the demand was there for a value-for-money sporting car, unlike GM's highly specialised Corvette. Eventually Ford brilliantly improvised the Mustang, taking most of its parts from ordinary production-line saloons, giving that most important of all ingredients — sheer

A 1954 Jaguar XK 120 drophead
16 **coupé**

driving fun. It was also developed over the years to achieve formidable performance. Meanwhile, General Motors quickly produced the Chevrolet Camaro and the Pontiac Firebird: the sports car battle had been joined.

The success of the North American 'muscle cars' opened the door for a two-seater coupé in a more classic mould. The manufacturer to identify the market and to commit to both large-scale production and to large-scale risk was Datsun; the result, the 240Z, was to become an outstanding success. Back in Europe, designers were rethinking sports car layout and the fundamental change was to position the engine amidships, aft of the cabin but forward of the driven rear wheels. Some of the cars that appeared in this configuration were the Ferrari Dino, Fiat X1/9 and Lancia Stratos, but these did not convince Porsche, Datsun and Alfa Romeo, who continued to avoid the mid-engine layout.

When the fuel crisis reached its peak in the 1970s, the demise of the sports car was widely predicted, and some well-known marques did disappear, but basically it has survived to flourish at all levels, from the cheap sporty version of a sedan to what for most of us are the unaffordable sheer luxury supercars capable of speeds nearing 322km/h (200mph).

America's most popular sports car,
GM's Corvette

Alfa Romeo Spider Veloce

Country of origin: Italy
Date: first launched at Geneva Motor Show 1966, as the Duetto
Identity: small two-seater with 2-litre engine, no right-hand drive available from factory
Engine: front-mounted longitudinal four-cylinder with twin chain-driven ohc and Bosch Motronic ML 4.1 ignition/injection system; power 94kW (128PS) at 5,800rpm
Gears: five-speed manual; automatic not available; rear-wheel drive
Capacity: 1,962cc
Bore and stroke: 84 × 88.5mm (3.31 × 3.48in)
Maximum speed: 190km/h (118mph); 0 to 100km/h (62mph) 9.4sec; fuel tank 46 litres (10.1 Imp gal/12.12 USA gal)
Dimensions: wheelbase 2.25m (7ft 4.6in); length 4.25m (13ft 11.6in); width 1.63m (5ft 4.2in); height 1.29m (4ft 2.8in)
Chassis: front suspension independent wishbones and coil springs, anti-roll bar; rear live axle on longitudinal links with central wishbone
Brakes: solid discs front and rear; ABS not available
Tyres: 195/60 HR 15
Kerb weight: 1,110kg (2,447lb)

The latest Spider now has a one-piece bumper and grille opening, and full-width tail lights and one-piece bumper assembly at the back

Aston Martin V8 Vantage

Country of origin: UK
Date: introduced in 1981
Identity: the Vantage is a big 2+2 coupé, superbly finished, with luxury leather trimmings
Engine: front-mounted longitudinal V8-cylinder with two ohc per bank; four Weber 48 IDF/3 carburettors
Gears: five-speed manual standard; three-speed automatic available; rear-wheel drive
Capacity: 5,340cc
Bore and stroke: 100 × 85mm (3.94 × 3.35in)
Maximum speed: 270km/h (168mph); 0 to 97km/h (60mph) 5.2sec
Dimensions:: wheelbase 2.81m (9ft 2.8in); length 4.95m (16ft 2.8in); width 1.95m (6ft 4.8in); height 1.32m (4ft 4in)
Chassis: front suspension independent unequal length wishbones, coaxial coil springs, telescopic dampers and anti-roll bar; rear independent de Dion axle located by parallel trailing arms and transverse Watts linkage, coil springs, telescopic dampers and anti-roll bar
Brakes: vented discs front and rear; ABS not available
Tyres: 225/60 ZR 16
Kerb weight: 1,977kg (4,350lb)

Superb on the open road but not so good in traffic or at low speeds. It also suffers from having a large turning circle

Aston Martin Virage Volante

Country of origin: UK
Date: first launched 1988; convertible 1990
Identity: a luxurious grand tourer, though not at its best in traffic or at low speeds
Engine: front-mounted longitudinal V8-cylinder with twin chain-driven ohc working four valves per cylinder; Weber Marelli fuel injection; power 246kW (334PS) at 6,000rpm
Gears: five-speed manual; three-speed automatic available; rear-wheel drive
Capacity: 5,340cc
Bore and stroke: 100 × 85mm (3.94 × 3.35in)
Maximum speed: 252km/h (157mph); 0 to 97km/h (60mph) 6.8sec
Dimensions: wheelbase 2.61m (8ft 6.8in); length 4.74m (15ft 6.8in); width 1.85m (6ft 0.8in); height 1.32m (4ft 4in)
Chassis: front suspension independent wishbones, coil springs and anti-roll bar; rear de Dion axle with Watts linkage and triangulated radius arms, dual rate springs and damper units
Brakes: vented discs front; solid discs rear; ABS not available
Tyres: 225/60 ZR 16
Kerb weight: 1,790kg (3,946lb)

The two-door, four-passenger coupé appeared in 1988, first followed by the two-seat convertible Volante, and in 1992 Aston Martin announced the 2+2 Virage Volante

24

Audi V8 Quattro

Country of origin: Germany
Date: launched at Paris Motor Show, 1988
Identity: a sports sedan invader of a luxury sedan market, the V8 specification is magnificent
Engine: front-mounted longitudinal V8-cylinder with twin ohc, each bank working four valves per cylinder; all-alloy construction with Bosch Motronic injection/ignition system; power 184kW (250PS) at 5,800rpm
Gears: automatic four-speed; manual transmission not available; four-wheel drive
Capacity: 3,562cc
Bore and stroke: 81 × 86.4mm (3.19 × 3.4in)
Maximum speed: 232km/h (144mph); 0 to 97km/h (60mph) 9sec
Dimensions: wheelbase 2.7m (8ft 10.3in); length 4.81m (15ft 11.3in); width 1.81m (5ft 11.4in); height 1.42m (4ft 7.9in)
Chassis: front suspension independent MacPherson struts and anti-roll bar; rear independent trailing arms, coil springs and anti-roll bar
Brakes: vented discs front and rear; ABS standard
Tyres: 215/60 VR 15
Kerb weight: 1,710kg (3,770lb)

By virtue of its all-wheel-drive system, the V8 is the flagship of the Audi line and is perhaps the most complete of all high-priced touring sedans currently available

BMW 535i Sport

Country of origin: Germany
Date: launched in 1989
Identity: BMW's benchmark sports sedan
Engine: front-mounted longitudinal six-cylinder with alloy head and single ohc working 12 valves; Bosch Motronic system; power 157kW (211PS) at 5,700 rpm
Gears: five-speed manual; four speed automatic available; rear-wheel drive
Capacity: 3,430cc
Bore and stroke: 92 × 86mm (3.62 × 3.39in)
Maximum speed: 227km/h (141mph); 0 to 97km/h (60mph) 7.4sec
Dimensions: wheelbase 2.76m (9ft 0.7in); length 4.72m (15ft 5.8in); width 1.75m (5ft 8.9in); height 1.41m (4ft 7.6in)
Chassis: front suspension independent double-jointed spring struts with anti-drive and self-compensating features, and anti-roll bar; rear independent semi-trailing arms with auxiliary trailing arms featuring anti-drive and anti-squat geometry, coil springs and anti-roll bar
Brakes: vented disks front and rear; ABS standard
Tyres: 240/45 ZR 415
Kerb weight: 1,525kg (3,362lb)

The 525i models are pre-wired for alarm systems and telephone controls. The limited production M5 has Servotronic power steering

BMW 850i

Country of origin: Germany
Date: launched at Frankfurt in 1989
Identity: this sleek four-seater, two-door sports
coupé was built to replace the 635 CSi range; the
8-series is expected to develop a full range
Engine: front-mounted longitudinal V12
cylinder with alloy block and heads, single
chain-driven ohc per bank and hydraulic tappets;
Bosch Motronic injection/ignition system;
power 224kW (300PS) at 5,200rpm
Gears: six-speed manual; four-speed automatic
optional; rear-wheel drive
Capacity: 4,988cc
Bore and stroke: 84 × 75mm (3.3 × 2.95in)
Maximum speed: 253km/h (157mph); 0 to
97km/h (60mph) 7.2sec
Dimensions: wheelbase 2.68m (8ft 9.6in);
length 4.78m (15ft 8.1in); width 1.85m (6ft
1in); height 1.34m (4ft 4.8in)
Chassis: front suspension independent double
jointed spring struts with anti-drive, self
compensating features and anti-roll bar; rear
independent five-link layout with coil springs,
anti-drive, anti-squat and anti-roll bar
Brakes: vented discs front; solid discs rear; ABS
standard
Tyres: 235/50 ZR 16
Kerb weight: 1,790kg (3,946lb)

30   *Ellipsoid pop-up headlamps and a*
compressed nose show the ancestry

BMW Z1

Country of origin: Germany
Date: announced at Frankfurt 1987; entered production 1988 but production ceased in 1991
Identity: little two-seater sports car with body-work in composite
Engine: front-mounted longitudinal six-cylinder with belt-driven ohc and inclined valves in hemi-head; Bosch Motronic injection/ignition system; power 125kW (170PS) at 5,800rpm
Gears: five-speed manual; automatic not available; rear-wheel drive
Capacity: 2,494cc
Bore and stroke: 84 × 75mm (3.3 × 2.95in)
Maximum speed: 219km/h (136mph); 0 to 97km/h (60mph) 7.9sec
Dimensions: wheelbase 2.45m (8ft 0.5in) length 3.92m (12ft 10.3in); width 1.69m (5ft 6.5in); height 1.27m (4ft 2.3in)
Chassis: front suspension independent Mac-Pherson struts and anti-roll bar; rear independent trailing and semi-trailing arms, coil springs, telescopic dampers and anti-roll bar
Brakes: vented discs front; solid discs rear; ABS standard
Tyres: 205/55 VR 15
Kerb weight: 1,100kg (2,425lb)

The small doors of the Z1 open downwards into the sills. Pop-up headlamps are featured and the engine is positioned well back

Buick Regal Gran Sport

Country of origin: USA
Date: the specification given below is for 1991
Identity: two-door, four-passenger coupé
Engine: front-mounted longitudinal V6-cylinder ohv; supercharger; power 125kW (170PS) at 4,800rpm
Gears: four-speed automatic only; front-wheel drive
Capacity: 3.8 litres
Maximum speed: 193km/h (120mph)
Dimensions: wheelbase 2.73m (8ft 11.5in); length 4.92m (16ft 1.6in); width 1.84m (6ft 0.5in); height 1.34m (4ft 5in); front track 1.51m (4ft 11.5in); rear track 1.47m (4ft 10in)
Chassis: front suspension independent Mac Pherson struts and coil springs; rear independent three-link struts and transverse mono-leaf spring
Brakes: vented discs front; solid discs rear; ABS optional
Tyres: 225/60 R 16 Eagle GA blackwalls
Kerb weight: 1,471kg (3,236lb)

The range of Regals includes the Custom, the Limited and the Gran Sport, all of which are available in both three and four-door body styles Equipped with power-assisted rack and pinion steering and lubed-for-life DynaRide suspension; a 3.1-litre V6 engine is also optional

Buick Reatta convertible

Country of origin: USA
Date: the Reatta convertible was added to the range in 1990
Identity: a neat two-seater; the hood has a rigid hinged cover, with electric release
Engine: front-mounted transverse V6-cylinder with alloy heads and central chain-driven camshaft operating hydraulic tappets; sequential fuel injection; power 123kW (167PS) at 4,800rpm
Gears: five-speed automatic; front-wheel drive
Capacity: 3,785cc
Bore and stroke: 96.5 × 86.4mm (3.8 × 3.4in)
Maximum speed: 193km/h (120mph)
Dimensions: wheelbase 2.5m (8ft 2.5in); length 4.66m (15ft 3.7in); width 1.85m (6ft 1in); height 1.3m (4ft 3.2in)
Chassis: front suspension independent Mac-Pherson struts and anti-roll bar; rear independent modular assembly with single transverse leaf spring, deflected disc dampers and anti-roll bar
Brakes: solid discs front and rear
Tyres: P215/65 R 15
Kerb weight: 1,615kg (3,562lb)

The 1991 coupé shown right had restyled wheels and analogue instrumentation but with switchable speedometer reading; other features include air bags as standard

Cadillac Allanté

Country of origin: USA
Date: the 4.5-litre engine introduced 1989
Identity: an aluminium and galvanised steel-bodied two-seater with hood and hard top
Engine: front-mounted transverse V8-cylinder with alloy block and heads, cast-iron cylinder liners, pushrod valve gear and hydraulic tappets, electronic sequential port fuel injection; power 149kW (203PS) at 4,300rpm
Gears: automatic four-speed standard; manual not available; front-wheel drive
Capacity: 4,467cc
Bore and stroke: 92 × 84mm (3.62 × 3.3in)
Maximum speed: 185km/h (115mph); 0 to 97km/h (60mph) 8.5sec
Dimensions: wheelbase 2.52m (8ft 2.4in) length 4.54m (14ft 10.6in); width 1.86m (6ft 1.5in); height 1.33m (4ft 4.2in)
Chassis: front suspension independent MacPherson struts with lateral and trailing links and anti-roll bar; rear independent struts, H-control arms, transverse composite leaf spring and telescopic dampers
Brakes: vented discs front; solid discs rear; ABS standard
Tyres: P225/55 VR 16 Goodyear Eagle
Kerb weight: 1,584kg (3,492lb)

Bodies built by Pininfarina are flown to America for the running gear to be fitted

38

Chevrolet Beretta

Country of origin: USA
Date: the range remains in production, upgraded for 1992
Identity: a two-door coupé
Engine: front-mounted longitudinal V6-cylinder ohv with multi-port fuel injection; power 80kW (110PS) at 5,200rpm
Gears: three-speed automatic; five-speed manual available; ABS VI braking system from 1992; front-wheel drive
Capacity: 3.1 litres
Maximum speed: 200km/h (124mph)
Dimensions: wheelbase 2.62m (8ft 8.4in); length 4.66m (15ft 3.4in); width 1.73m (5ft 8.2in); height 1.42m (4ft 8.2in)
Chassis: front suspension independent Mac-Pherson struts, coil springs and lower control arms; rear semi-independent beam axle, trailing arms and coil springs
Brakes: vented discs front; drums rear
Tyres: 205/55 R 16
Kerb weight: 1,205kg (2,649lb)

Beretta models include the GT2 with automatic transmission and detailed above, and the 252 Corsica/FE3 Beretta Sport package, both with a new cylinder head for 1992

Chevrolet Camaro Z-28

Country of origin: USA
Date: the Z-28 first appeared in 1972; continually refined and updated, 1993 will see yet another new version
Identity: two-door 2 + 2 coupé
Engine: front-mounted longitudinal V8-cylinder with alloy head and blocks, twin ohc, each bank working four valves per cylinder; Multec fuel injection; power 180kW (245PS) at 4,400rpm
Gears: four-speed automatic; five-speed manual available; both versions have overdrive top gear; rear-wheel drive
Capacity: 5.7 litres
Maximum speed: 201km/h (125mph); 0 to 97km/h (60mph) 5.8sec
Dimensions: wheelbase 2.56m (8ft 5in); length 4.89m (16ft 0.6in); width 1.84m (6ft 0.4in); height 1.28m (4ft 2.4in)
Chassis: front suspension independent MacPherson struts, coil springs and anti-roll bar; rear independent live axle, track bar, torque arm and coil springs
Brakes: vented discs front; drums rear; ABS not available
Tyres: 225/60 VR 16
Kerb weight: 1,410kg (3,103lb)

The Camaro is also available as the RS coupé, and both versions are available with convertible tops.

Chevrolet Corvette LT1 convertible

Country of origin: USA
Date: the LT1 is the convertible version of the ZR-1, with late-1980s styling
Identity: the 1991 model is fitted with four horizontal louvres behind the front wheel arch
Engine: front-mounted longitudinal V8-cylinder with alloy heads and block, twin ohc each bank working four valves per cylinder Multec fuel injection; power 279kW (380PS) at 5,800rpm
Gears: six-speed manual; automatic not available; rear-wheel drive
Capacity: 5,736cc
Bore and stroke: 99 × 93mm (3.89 × 3.66)
Maximum speed: 283km/h (176mph); 0 to 97km/h (60mph) 5.6sec
Dimensions: wheelbase 2.44m (8ft 0.2in), length 4.53m (14ft 10.5in); width 1.86m (6ft 1.2in); height 1.18m (3ft 10.7in)
Chassis: front suspension independent wishbones, transverse glass-fibre reinforced plastic leaf spring and anti-roll bar; rear independent five-link location with transverse glass-fibre plastic leaf spring and anti-roll bar
Brakes: vented discs front and rear; ABS standard
Tyres: front 275/40 ZR 17; rear 315/35 ZR 17
Kerb weight: 1,571kg (3,465lb)

The new small-block V8 engine features reverse-flow cooling

Chevrolet Geo Storm GSi

Country of origin: Japan/Canada
Date: introduced in the late 1980s, the current range now includes a 2 + 2 coupé, the GSi and, from 1991, a hatchback model
Identity: a two-wheel drive version of the Geo Tracker sport, the Geo Storm is produced in Japan and assembled in Canada
Engine: front-mounted transverse four-cylinder with alloy head and single ohc, working three valves per cylinder; Multec fuel injection; power 85kW (116PS) at 4,800rpm
Gears: five-speed manual; four-speed automatic available; front-wheel drive
Capacity: 1,769cc
Bore and stroke: 80 × 79mm (3.15 × 3.11in)
Maximum speed: 169km/h (105mph)
Dimensions: wheelbase 2.45m (8ft 0.5in); length 4.15m (13ft 8.4in); width 1.69m (5ft 6.7in); height 1.3m (4ft 3.1in)
Chassis: front suspension independent MacPherson struts and anti-roll bar; rear independent MacPherson struts
Brakes: solid discs front; drums rear; ABS not available
Tyres: 205/50 VR 15 Gatorback
Kerb weight: 1,035kg (2,262lb)

The 1992 GSi version illustrated right features electric windows and central locking as standard, and a
46 *driver's air-bag restraint*

Chevrolet Lumina

Country of origin: USA
Date: details below are for the 1992 Lumina Z34 coupé
Identity: two-door coupé with big interior, to seat five
Engine: front-mounted longitudinal V6-cylinder dohc; power 158kW (215PS) at 4,000rpm
Gears: three-speed or four-speed automatic; manual also available; front-wheel drive
Capacity: 3.4 litres
Maximum speed: 205km/h (127mph)
Dimensions: wheelbase 2.73m (8ft 11.5in); length 5.03m (16ft 6.3in); width 1.8m (5ft 11in); height 1.36m (4ft 5.5in)
Chassis: front suspension independent MacPherson struts, coil springs and shock absorbers; rear independent MacPherson struts and transverse leaf springs
Brakes: vented discs front; solid discs rear; ABS standard
Tyres: 225/60 R 16 Eagles
Kerb weight: 1,416kg (3,115lb)

The larger V6 engine was introduced in 1992 for both the Z34 and Euro (pictured right) models, together with the ABS VI braking system

Delorean DMC12

Country of origin: UK
Date: first available in 1980
Identity: a two-door coupé of fibreglass body structure, with unpainted stainless steel body panels and gullwing doors
Engine: a Peugeot-Renault-Volvo four-stroke engine mounted transversely behind the driver, six cylinders inline ohvs with two ohcs; power 96kW (130PS) at 5,500rpm
Gears: five-speed fully synchronised only
Capacity: 2,850cc
Bore and stroke: 91 × 73mm (3.58 × 2.87in)
Maximum speed: 209km/h (130mph)
Dimensions: wheelbase 2.41m (7ft 11in); front track 1.66m (5ft 5.4in); rear track 1.59m (5ft 2.7in)
Chassis: front suspension independent parallel unequal length upper and lower control arms, coil springs and coaxial telescopic dampers; rear independent trailing arms with upper and lower unequal length parallel transverse control arms, coil springs and coaxial telescopic dampers
Brakes: discs front and rear

Intended by John Z Delorean to break new ground in automotive technology, it was designed by Giorgetto Giugiaro. Complaints were numerous and only 40,000 units were built before the British Government called in the receiver in 1982

Dodge Daytona

Country of origin: USA
Date: first appeared in 1983; the IROC model, with V6 engine, was introduced in 1991
Identity: two-door, four-passenger hatchback
Engine: front-mounted transverse single ohc, turbocharger with intercooler; power 164kW (224PS) at 6,000rpm
Gears: three or four-speed automatic; five-speed manual available; front-wheel drive
Capacity: 2,213cc
Maximum speed: 220km/h (137mph); 0 to 97km/h (60mph) 6.7sec
Dimensions: wheelbase 2.47m (8ft 1.2in); length 4.57m (14ft 11.8in); width 1.76m (5ft 9.3in); height 1.31m (4ft 3.8in)
Chassis: front suspension independent MacPherson struts and coil springs; rear beam axle, trailing arms and coil springs
Brakes: vented discs front and rear; ABS standard
Tyres: 205/55 VR 16
Kerb weight: 1,263kg (2,779lb)

The 1980s Daytona illustrated opposite was available with 2.2 or 2.5-litre engines. Increased speed was obtained in 1987, when the intercooler was added. The IROC R/T has a balance-shaft 2.2-litre dohc, producing higher output than any Chrysler production engine

52

Dodge Stealth R/T Turbo

Country of origin: USA
Date: little change from its 1991 specification
Identity: available are the base Stealth with a 12V 3-litre V6 engine, ES, R/T and R/T Turbo; only the Turbo has four-wheel drive and steering system; all two-door 2 + 2 hatchbacks
Engine: front-mounted longitudinal V6-cylinder with 24 valves; turbocharger with twin intercooler; power 148kW (201PS) at 4,500rpm
Gears: four-speed automatic; five-speed manual available; four-wheel drive
Capacity: 3 litres
Maximum speed: 209km/h (130mph); 0 to 97km/h (60mph) 4.9sec
Dimensions: wheelbase 2.47m (8ft 1.2in); length 4.58m (15ft 0.2in); width 1.84m (6ft 0.4in); height 1.25m (4ft 1.1in); front track 1.56m (5ft 1.4in); rear track 1.58m (5ft 2.2in)
Chassis: front suspension independent Mac-Pherson struts and coil springs; rear independent double wishbones, trailing arms, dual links and coil springs
Brakes: vented discs front and rear; ABS standard
Tyres: 225/55 VR 16
Kerb weight: 1,402kg (3,086lb)

Electronic variable damping with touring and sports settings are available on the R/T Turbo model; illustrated right is the ES

54

Dodge Viper RT/10

Country of origin: USA
Date: limited production from early 1992
Identity: two-door, two-seat roadster
Engine: front-mounted longitudinal V10-cylinder pushrod ohv with alloy block and heads electronic fuel injection; power 294kW (400PS) at 5,500rpm
Gears: six-speed Borg-Warner manual; rear-wheel drive
Capacity: 8 litres
Maximum speed: 233km/h (145mph) estimated
Dimensions: wheelbase 2.44m (8ft 0.6in) length 4.45m (14ft 7.1in)
Chassis: front suspension double A-arm, tube shocks and coil springs; rear independent double A-arms, tube shocks and coil springs
Brakes: vented discs front and rear; ABS not available
Tyres: front Michelin P275/40 ZR 17; rear P335/35 ZR 17
Kerb weight: 1,491kg (3,280lb)

The Viper body is made in several large pieces fastened mechanically into a complete shell, with the enormous hood section separating just above the headlamps and at the cowl. The front fenders are open at their after-ends as vents for the under-hood air and to cool the electronics

Eagle Talon TSi

Country of origin: USA
Date: the 1992 models look considerably different to their predecessors, with new front and rear fascias, front fenders, hood, tail lamps and spoiler
Identity: two-door, four-passenger coupé
Engine: front-mounted longitudinal dohc four-cylinder; turbocharger with intercooler; power 143kW (195PS) at 6,000rpm
Gears: five-speed manual with overdrive; four-speed automatic available; four-wheel drive
Capacity: 2 litres
Maximum speed: 185km/h (115mph)
Dimensions: wheelbase 2.47m (8ft 1.2in); length 4.38m (14ft 4.4in); width 1.7m (5ft 6.9in); height 1.3m (4ft 3.4in); front track 1.47m (4ft 9.7in); rear track 1.45m (4ft 9.3in)
Chassis: front suspension MacPherson struts, control arms and coil springs; rear beam axle, three-links, torsion bars and double wishbones
Brakes: vented discs front; solid discs rear; ABS optional
Tyres: P225/60 VR 16
Kerb weight: 1,232kg (2,712lb)

Gone are the pop-up headlamps for 1992, in favour of flush mounting. A new ergonomically designed instrument panel and controls are other new features

Ferrari 246 GT Dino

Country of origin: Italy
Date: introduced as the 206 GT Dino in 1968, it was uprated to the 246 in the following year
Identity: produced in closed GT and open GTS forms as a two-door, two-seat, smaller Ferrari, styled by Pininfarina
Engine: mid-mounted 65° V6-cylinder with twin ohcs per bank; three Weber carburettors; power 143kW (195PS) at 7,600rpm
Gears: five-speed manual only; rear-wheel drive
Capacity: 2,418cc
Bore and stroke: 92.5 × 60mm (3.64 × 2.36in)
Maximum speed: 213km/h (133mph)
Dimensions: wheelbase 2.34m (7ft 8in); front track 1.42m (4ft 8in); rear track 1.4m (4ft 7in)
Chassis: steel tubular and sheet; front suspension independent wishbones, coil springs, dampers and anti-roll bars; rear independent wishbones, coil springs, dampers and anti-roll bars
Brakes: vented discs front and rear

It was the cheapest Ferrari ever built, and, with 3,761 being made between 1969-1974, was more extensively sold than any previous Ferrari. It was mechanically excellent, looked good and performed superbly. It was replaced by the larger 208 and 308 GT4 models in 1973, with their new 2 or 3-litre V8 engines and 2+2 seating

60

Ferrari 308 GTO

Country of origin: Italy
Date: 272 were made between 1984-1985
Identity: aimed at competitions, and only superficially similar to the 308 GTB, sharing few components apart from the steel doors
Engine: mid-mounted longitudinal V8-cylinder four ohc, working four valves per cylinder; twin turbocharger; Weber-Marelli electronic injection/ignition; power 294kW (400PS) at 7,000rpm
Gears: five-speed manual only; rear-wheel drive
Capacity: 2,855cc
Bore and stroke: 80 × 71mm (3.15 × 2.8in)
Maximum speed: 301km/h (187mph); 0 to 100km/h (62mph) 4.9sec
Dimensions: wheelbase 2.45m (8ft 0.5in); front and rear tracks 1.56m (5ft 1.4in)
Chassis: an all-new spaceframe of tubular steel; front suspension independent with Koni hydraulic shock absorbers, coaxial springs and stabiliser bar; rear independent Koni hydraulic shock absorbers, coaxial springs and stabiliser bar
Brakes: vented discs front and rear
Tyres: front 225/55 VR 16; rear 265/50 VR 16

A sleek, stylish Pininfarina-designed two-seat Berlinetta, with body panels of carbon fibre, fibreglass or Kevlar, covering a standing 400m (quarter-mile) in 12.7sec

Ferrari 348 tb

Country of origin: Italy
Date: introduced at Frankfurt in 1988
Identity: two-seat, two-door targa
Engine: mid-mounted longitudinal V8-cylinder with alloy block and cylinder heads, twin ohc each bank working four valves per cylinder; Bosch Motronic injection; power 221kW (300PS) at 7,200rpm
Gears: five-speed manual only; rear-wheel drive
Capacity: 3,405cc
Bore and stroke: 85 × 75mm (3.35 × 2.95in)
Maximum speed: 262km/h (163mph); 0 to 97km/h (60mph) 5.6sec
Dimensions: wheelbase 2.45m (8ft 0.5in); length 4.23m (13ft 10.5in); width 1.89m (6ft 2.6in); height 1.17m (3ft 10in)
Chassis: front suspension independent wishbones, coil springs and anti-roll bar; rear independent wishbones, coil springs and anti-roll bar
Brakes: vented discs front and rear; ABS standard
Tyres: front 215/50 ZR 17; rear 255/45 ZR 17
Kerb weight: 1,393kg (3,070lb)

An improvement on the 328 GTB, which it replaced; the 348 has a longer wheelbase, thus improving the ride, and an underbody which allows the control pedals and steering wheel to be directly ahead of the driver

Ferrari 512 BB Berlinetta Boxer

Country of origin: Italy

Date: introduced in 1973, engine capacity increased 1976; then replaced by the Testarossa

Identity: Pininfarina two-door 2 + 2 coupé

Engine: mid-mounted longitudinal flat-12 twin ohcs per bank; four Weber triple-choke carburettors; power 250kW (340PS) at 6,800rpm

Gears: five-speed manual; automatic not available; rear-wheel drive

Capacity: 4,942cc

Bore and stroke: 82 × 78mm (3.23 × 3.07in)

Maximum speed: 270km/h (168mph); 0 to 97km/h (60mph) 6.5sec

Dimensions: wheelbase 2.5m (8ft 2.5in); front track 1.5m (4ft 11in); rear 1.51m (4ft 11.5in)

Chassis: tubular with monocoque centre section; front suspension independent wishbones, coil springs, dampers and anti-roll bar; rear independent wishbones, coil springs, dampers and anti-roll bar

Brakes: vented discs front and rear; ABS not available

Kerb weight: 1,743kg (3,836lb)

The 512 BB was Ferrari's first mid-engined street car; the more powerful 1976 model was wider and also had a nose-spoiler. Bosch Jetronic injection replaced the carburettors in 1981, and the model designated 512i

Ferrari Mondial t

Country of origin: Italy
Date: 1980; revised edition at Geneva in 1989
Identity: two-door 2 + 2 coupé; mildly flared wheel arches, flush-fitting body-colour door handles and restyled side air intakes
Engine: mid-mounted longitudinal V8-cylinder toothed belt drive, twin ohc each bank working four valves per cylinder; Bosch Motronic injection; power 221kW (300PS) at 7,000rpm
Gears: five-speed manual only; rear-wheel drive
Capacity: 3,405cc
Bore and stroke: 85 × 75mm (3.35 × 2.95in)
Maximum speed: 230km/h (143mph)
Dimensions: wheelbase 2.65m (8ft 8.3in); length 4.53m (14ft 10.5in); width 1.81m (5ft 11.2in); height 1.23m (4ft 0.6in)
Chassis: front suspension independent wishbones and coil springs, electrically adjusted shocks, anti-roll bar and three-position damper firmness control; rear independent, as front
Brakes: vented discs front and rear; ABS standard
Tyres: front 205/55 ZR 16; rear 225/55 ZR 16
Kerb weight: 1,468kg (3,236lb)

A smaller steering wheel, with power-assisted rack and pinion and new suspension placing the engine lower and with transverse transmission, are new features

68

Ferrari Testarossa

Country of origin: Italy
Date: the new Pininfarina was launched at Paris in 1984, and revived this 1960s spectacular
Identity: two-door, two-seat coupé, one of the world's fastest cars; *Automotor and Sport* claimed to have tested it at 291km/h (181mph)
Engine: mid-mounted longitudinal 12-cylinder with horizontal layout and toothed belt drive to twin ohc each bank working four valves per cylinder; Bosch KE Jetronic injection; power 291kW (390PS) at 6,300rpm
Gears: five-speed manual only; rear-wheel drive
Capacity: 4,942cc
Bore and stroke: 82 × 78mm (3.23 × 3.07in)
Maximum speed: 275km/h (171mph); 0 to 97km/h (60mph) 5.2sec
Dimensions: wheelbase 2.55m (8ft 4.4in); length 4.48m (14ft 8.6in); width 1.97m (6ft 5.8in); height 1.13m (3ft 8.5in)
Chassis: front suspension independent wishbones, coil springs and anti-roll bar; rear independent wishbones, coil springs and anti-roll bar
Brakes: vented discs front and rear; ABS not available
Tyres: front 225/50 ZR 16; rear 255/50 ZR 16
Kerb weight: 1,668kg (3,675lb)

The most exciting of cars, with
70 *formidable acceleration*

Fiat X1/9

Country of origin: Italy
Date: first announced in 1972, it was the first mass-produced mid-engined sports car
Identity: a neat sporty two-seat wedge-shaped package, based on a Bertone design
Engine: straight four single ohc, one Weber carburettor, mounted transversely behind the driver; power 62kW (85PS) at 6,000rpm
Gears: five-speed manual
Capacity: 1,498cc
Bore and stroke: 86 × 63.9mm (3.4 × 2.51in)
Maximum speed: 177km/h (110mph); 0 to 97km/h (60mph) 12.6sec
Dimensions: wheelbase 2.2m (7ft 2.5in); track 1.35m (4ft 5in)
Chassis: front suspension independent MacPherson struts and lower wishbones; rear independent MacPherson struts, wishbones and single links
Brakes: solid discs front and rear

The X1/9 was launched with the 1,290cc 55kW (75PS) 4-cylinder engine as used in the 128 saloon, and driving through a 128 gearbox. Not notably fast, the adoption of the 1,498cc Strada engine in 1977 gave a definite improvement; fun to drive, it handled well

Ford Mustang

Country of origin: USA
Date: a 1992 specification update on the original 1964, which is shown on the following pages
Identity: four-passenger, two-door coupé, convertible or hatchback
Engine: front-mounted longitudinal V8-cylinder with alloy block and heads, ohv; power 165kW (225PS) at 4,200rpm
Gears: four-speed automatic; five-speed manual available; rear-wheel drive
Capacity: 5 litres
Maximum speed: 201km/h (125mph)
Dimensions: wheelbase 2.55m (8ft 4.5in); length 4.56m (14ft 11.6in); width 1.73m (5ft 8.3in); height 1.32m (4ft 4.1in)
Chassis: front suspension independent MacPherson struts and coil springs; rear independent live axle, four links and coil springs
Brakes: vented discs front; drums rear; ABS not available
Tyres: 225/55 ZR 16 Eagle GT + 4
Kerb weight: 1,261kg (2,775lb)

The Mustang underwent great changes in the 1970s, to emerge in the 1980s as no longer the muscle car of its formative years; it will take more than the 1992 modifications to body-side mouldings and bumper strips to recreate the enthusiasm and following it once enjoyed

Ford Mustang GT

Country of origin: USA
Date: originated in 1964, when it became an instant best-seller; details below are for the 1964 model
Identity: four-passenger, two-door convertible
Engine: four-stroke, four cylinders inline, ohv; one downdraught twin-barrel carburettor; power 63kW (86PS) at 4,600rpm
Gears: four-speed fully synchronised manual
Capacity: 2,300cc
Bore and stroke: 95.9 × 79.5mm (3.77 × 3.13in)
Maximum speed: 154km/h (96mph)
Dimensions: wheelbase 2.55m (8ft 4.4in); front track 1.44m (4ft 8.6in), rear track 1.45m (4ft 9in)
Chassis: platform with front subframe; front suspension independent MacPherson struts, wishbones, lower control arms, coil springs, telescopic dampers and anti-roll bar; rear rigid axle, lower trailing radius arms, upper oblique torque arms, transverse linkage bar, coil springs and telescopic dampers
Brakes: solid discs front; drums rear

The Mustang won the Industrial Designers Institute Award and also the Tiffany Gold Medal Award, when in the Spring of 1964 thousands of people flocked to the salesrooms to 76 *buy this unusual new car*

Ford Probe LX

Country of origin: USA
Date: a basically new and substantially improved Probe was launched in the Spring of 1992
Identity: four-passenger, two-door hatchback built in Michigan, based on Mazda under-pinnings
Engine: front-mounted longitudinal Vulcan V6-cylinder ohv turbocharger with intercooler; power 118kW (160PS) at 3,000rpm
Gears: four-speed automatic; five-speed manual available; front-wheel drive
Capacity: 3 litres
Maximum speed: 185km/h (115mph)
Dimensions: wheelbase 2.51m (8ft 3in); length 4.49m (14ft 9in); width 1.72m (5ft 7.9in); height 1.31m (4ft 3.8in)
Chassis: front suspension independent Mac-Pherson struts, control arms and coil springs; rear independent four-bar wishbones, single trailing arms and coil springs
Brakes: vented discs front and rear; ABS optional
Tyres: 205/60 HR 15
Kerb weight: 1,241kg (2,730lb)

The new Probe includes both interior and exterior trim changes and some equipment deletions. The LX model detailed above includes a deck spoiler and alloy wheels

Ford Taurus SHO

Country of origin: USA
Date: the new 1992 range is another vastly altered model in the form of the SHO
Identity: the four-door, five-passenger standard Taurus LX is now a far cry from the features incorporated in the SHO
Engine: front-mounted longitudinal V6-cylinder 24-valve ohv; power 161.8kW (220PS) at 6,200rpm
Gears: four-speed automatic; five-speed manual available; front-wheel drive
Capacity: 3 litres
Maximum speed: 200km/h (124mph)
Dimensions: wheelbase 2.69m (8ft 10in); length 4.87m (16ft); width 1.8m (5ft 11.2in); height 1.37m (4ft 6.1in)
Chassis: front suspension independent MacPherson struts and coil springs; rear independent MacPherson struts, parallel arms, control arms and coil springs
Brakes: vented discs front; drums rear; ABS available
Tyres: 215/60 VR 16 Eagle GT + 4
Kerb weight: 1,423kg (3,131lb)

This popular Ford model has entirely new sheetmetal for 1992, excluding doors, a driver-oriented instrument panel, new seat and door trim, suspension changes and reduced noise and vibration

Ford Thunderbird SC

Country of origin: USA
Date: the 1989 edition was a substantially revised T-bird package
Identity: internally larger than previous Thunderbirds; identified by slats under front bumper
Engine: front-mounted longitudinal V6-cylinder with alloy heads and central chain-driven camshaft; Garrett turbocharger and intercooler; power 140kW (210PS) at 4,000rpm
Gears: five-speed manual; four-speed automatic available; rear-wheel drive
Capacity: 3,791cc
Bore and stroke: 96.5 × 86.4mm (3.8 × 3.4in)
Maximum speed: 210km/h (125mph)
Dimensions: wheelbase 2.87m (9ft 5in); length 5.05m (16ft 6.7in); width 1.85m (6ft 0.7in); height 1.34m (4ft 4.7in)
Chassis: front suspension independent wishbones and struts, coil springs, gas-filled telescopic dampers and anti-roll bar; rear independent lower H-arm and upper arms, coil springs, gas-filled telescopic dampers and anti-roll bar
Brakes: solid discs front and rear; ABS standard
Tyres: P225/60 VR 16
Kerb weight: 1,607kg (3,542lb)

The 1989 Super Coupé illustrated right remains in production with very little alteration apart from a smaller fuel tank

Ginetta G33

Country of origin: UK
Date: 1991 specification for this limited-production V8 roadster
Identity: high-performance two-door light-weight convertible
Engine: front-mounted longitudinal V8-cylinder with alloy head and block; electronic fuel injection; power 149kW (203PS) at 5,280rpm
Gears: five-speed manual; rear-wheel drive
Capacity: 3,947cc
Bore and stroke: 94×71.1mm (3.7×2.8in)
Maximum speed: 233km/h (145mph); 0 to 97km/h (60mph) 5sec
Dimensions: wheelbase 2.16m (7ft 1in); length 3.54m (11ft 7.6in); width 1.47m (4ft 9.8in); height 1.01m (3ft 3.9in)
Chassis: glass-reinforced polyester resin on galvanised steel chassis; front suspension independent wishbones, coil springs and anti-roll bar; rear independent lower wishbones, longitudinal links and fixed length drive shafts, coil springs and anti-roll bar
Brakes: vented discs front, solid discs rear; ABS not available
Tyres: 195/50 ZR 15
Kerb weight: 680kg (1,500lb)

The luxury interior includes leather trim and pile carpet. Headlamps pop up from a single-piece section

Honda Beat

Country of origin: Japan
Date: the original S600 appeared in the early 1960s; the Beat was launched in 1992
Identity: two-seat convertible
Engine: mid-mounted transverse three-cylinder inline; 12 valves; MTREC (multi-throttle responsive engine control system); electronic ignition and fuel injection; power 47kW (64PS) at 8,100rpm
Gears: five-speed manual; rear-wheel drive
Capacity: 656cc
Bore and stroke: 66 × 64mm (2.6 × 2.5in)
Maximum speed: 0 to 97km/h (60mph) 10sec
Dimensions: wheelbase 2.28m (7ft 5.8in); length 3.29m (10ft 9.7in); width 1.39m (4ft 6.9in); front and rear track 1.21m (3ft 11.6in)
Chassis: front suspension independent MacPherson struts, lower A-arms, coil springs, dampers and anti-roll bar; rear independent MacPherson struts, coil springs, dampers, radius rod, trailing links and twin lateral links
Brakes: discs front and rear
Tyres: front 155/65 R 13; 165/60 R 14 rear
Kerb weight: 761kg (1,675lb)

The Honda Beat captures all the fun of small open-top sports car motoring with the very latest in technology, designed with an extensive list of standard equipment and a host of optional extras available

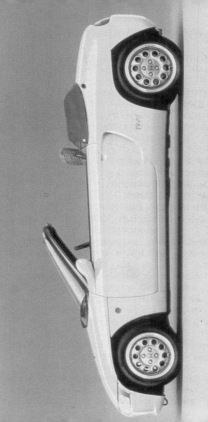

Honda CRX 1.6i-VT

Country of origin: Japan
Date: revised to its current specification in 1990; a larger-engined version from Spring 1992
Identity: a 2 + 2 sporting coupé based on the Civic range
Engine: front-mounted transverse four-cylinder with alloy head and twin ohc working four valves per cylinder, with automatic control of valve timing and lift; Honda PGM electronic fuel injection; power 110kW (150PS) at 7,800rpm
Gears: five-speed manual; automatic not available; front-wheel drive
Capacity: 1,596cc
Bore and stroke: 81 × 77mm (3.19 × 3.03in)
Maximum speed: 209km/h (130mph); 0 to 97km/h (60mph) 8sec
Dimensions: wheelbase 2.3m (7ft 6.5in); length 3.75m (12ft 4.6in); width 1.6m (5ft 5.9in); height 1.27m (4ft 2in)
Chassis: front suspension independent wishbones and coil springs and anti-roll bar; rear independent wishbones and coil springs and anti-roll bar
Brakes: vented discs front, solid discs rear; ABS standard
Tyres: 195/60 VR 14
Kerb weight: 1,025kg (2,258lb)

A compact coupé offering excellent economy, though only reasonable equipment

Honda Legend coupé

Country of origin: Japan
Date: all-new Legend introduced in 1991
Identity: a two-door, four-seat coupé, larger and more rounded than previous models
Engine: front-mounted longitudinal V6-cylinder with all-alloy construction and single ohc per bank working four valves per cylinder; distributorless ignition; power 205kW (279PS) at 5,500rpm
Gears: five-speed manual; four-speed automatic available; four-wheel drive
Capacity: 3,206cc
Bore and stroke: 90 × 84mm (3.54 × 3.31in)
Maximum speed: 226km/h (140mph); 0 to 100km/h (62mph) 8.1sec
Dimensions: wheelbase 2.91m (9ft 6.6in); length 4.88m (16ft 0.3in); width 1.81m (5ft 11.3in); height 1.37m (4ft 5.9in)
Chassis: front suspension independent wishbones and coil springs with lateral arms and anti-roll bar; rear independent wishbones and coil springs with lateral arms and anti-roll bar
Brakes: vented discs front; solid discs rear; ABS standard
Tyres: 205/65 ZR 15
Kerb weight: 1,545kg (3,406lb)

The new Legend has the engine placed longitudinally instead of transversely, and comes with many more refinements

Honda NSX

Country of origin: Japan
Date: a new car for the 1990s
Identity: a stunning high-performance GT
Engine: mid-mounted transverse V6-cylinder with twin ohc, each bank working four valves per cylinder with varying valve timing; programmed electronic ignition with varying volume induction system; power 201kW (273PS) at 7,300rpm
Gears: five-speed manual; automatic available; rear-wheel drive
Capacity: 2,977cc
Bore and stroke: 90 × 78mm (3.54 × 3.07in)
Maximum speed: 256km/h (159mph); 0 to 97km/h (60mph) 5.8sec
Dimensions: wheelbase 2.53m (8ft 0.6in); length 4.4m (14ft 5.4in); width 1.81m (5ft 11in); height 1.17m (3ft 10.1in)
Chassis: front suspension independent aluminium wishbones and coil springs, anti-roll bar; rear independent aluminium wishbones and coil springs, anti-roll bar
Brakes: vented discs front and rear; ABS standard
Tyres: front 205/50 ZR 15; rear 225/50 ZR 16
Kerb weight: 1,370kg (3,020lb)

This sleek new sports car offers electrically-operated power steering on automatic models, excellent roadholding and exciting acceleration

Honda Prelude

Country of origin: Japan
Date: a 1987 introduction for the Ex 2.0i, with the S and Si versions being introduced in 1993
Identity: two-door 2 + 2 passenger coupé
Engine: front-mounted transverse four-cylinder with twin ohc working 16 valves, an all-alloy construction and electronic PGM-FI fuel injection; power 110kW (150PS) at 6,000rpm
Gears: five-speed manual; four-speed automatic available; front-wheel drive
Capacity: 1,958cc
Bore and stroke: 81 × 95mm (3.19 × 3.74in)
Maximum speed: 206km/h (128mph); 0 to 97km/h (60mph) 8.5sec
Dimensions: wheelbase 2.56m (8ft 5in); length 4.46m (14ft 7.5in); width 1.69m (5ft 6.7in); height 1.29m (4ft 3in)
Chassis: front suspension independent wishbones, coil springs, telescopic dampers and anti-roll bar; rear independent wishbones and coil springs, telescopic dampers and anti-roll bar
Brakes: vented discs front; solid discs rear; ABS standard
Tyres: 195/60 VR 14
Kerb weight: 1,145kg (2,524lb)

Featuring all-wheel steering which produces excellent handling, both the S and Si models have engines based on the Accord 2.2-litre

Jaguar XJ6

Country of origin: UK
Date: the 3.2-litre 24-valve engine, 1990
Identity: the four-door, five-seat sedan with sports extras had new wheels and tyres for 1991
Engine: front-mounted longitudinal six-cylinder with alloy head and block, twin ohc working four valves per cylinder; Lucas fuel injection and ignition; power 149kW (203PS) at 5,250rpm
Gears: five-speed manual; four-speed automatic available; rear-wheel drive
Capacity: 3,239cc
Bore and stroke: 91 × 83mm (3.58 × 3.27in)
Maximum speed: 217km/h (135mph); 0 to 97km/h (60mph) 8.3sec
Dimensions: wheelbase 2.87m (9ft 5in); length 4.99m (16ft 4.4in); width 1.81m (5ft 11.3in); height 1.38m (4ft 6.3in)
Chassis: front suspension independent unequal length wishbones giving anti-drive effect, coil springs and anti-roll bar; rear independent wishbones with drive shafts as upper links, with anti-squat, anti-lift geometry, concentric coil springs and dampers
Brakes: vented discs front, solid discs rear; ABS standard
Tyres: 225/65 VR 15
Kerb weight: 1,800kg (3,969lb)

Jaguar introduced the 3.2 as the partner to the 4-litre

Jaguar XJS

Country of origin: UK
Date: the full convertible model was launched at
Geneva in 1988
Identity: a luxury handcrafted two-door con-
vertible with power hood
Engine: front-mounted longitudinal V12-
cylinder with all-alloy construction and single
ohc; Lucas digital fuel injection; power 217kW
(291PS) at 5,500rpm
Gears: three-speed automatic; manual available; rear-wheel drive
Capacity: 5,345cc
Bore and stroke: 90 × 70mm (3.54 × 2.75in)
Maximum speed: 232km/h (144mph); 0 to
97km/h (60mph) 8sec
Dimensions: wheelbase 2.59m (8ft 6in)
length 4.76m (15ft 7.6in); width 1.79m (5ft
10.6in); height 1.26m (4ft 1.7in)
Chassis: front suspension independent wishbones with anti-drive geometry, coil springs and
anti-roll bar; rear independent lower transverse
wishbones, driveshafts serve as upper links with
radius arms and coil springs
Brakes: vented discs front; solid discs rear; ABS
standard
Tyres: 235/60 VR15
Kerb weight: 1,835kg (4,055lb)

*One of the world's fastest open cars,
giving wonderful open-top motoring,
also available in coupé form*

Jaguar XJ220

Country of origin: UK
Date: V12 prototype 1988; first deliveries of a
limited edition of 220 were delivered in late 1991
Identity: definitely a luxury car
Engine: mid-mounted longitudinal V6-cylinder
with all-alloy construction, twin ohc working
four valves per cylinder, and twin water-cooled
turbochargers; electronic fuel injection; power
373kW (500PS) at 6,500rpm
Gears: five-speed manual only; rear-wheel
drive
Capacity: 3,498cc
Bore and stroke: 94 × 84mm (3.7 × 3.3in)
Maximum speed: 322 + km/h (200mph); 0 to
97km/h (60mph) 4sec
Dimensions: wheelbase 2.64m (8ft 8in)
length 4.86m (15ft 11in); width 2m (6ft 7in)
height 1.15m (3ft 9in)
Chassis: front suspension independent wish
bones, coil springs with concentric dampers and
anti-roll bar; rear independent wishbones, coil
springs, concentric damper units mounted trans
versely, toe control links and anti-roll bar
Brakes: vented discs front and rear; ABS
standard
Tyres: front 245/40 ZR 17; rear 345/35 ZR 18
Kerb weight: 1,560kg (3,448lb)

*This fast and luxurious sports model
will go back into production with
some amendments*

100

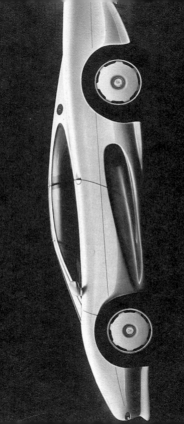

Lamborghini Countach

Country of origin: Italy
Date: first shown at Geneva in 1971, but not put into production until 1974
Identity: Lamborghini's successor to the Miura; the dramatic body was styled by Bertone with large doors, which opened up and forwards
Engine: mid-mounted longitudinal V12-cylinder four ohc; six Weber 4DCOE 104-105 twin-choke carburettors; power 275kW (375PS) at 8,000rpm
Gears: five-speed manual; rear-wheel drive
Capacity: 3,929cc
Bore and stroke: 82 × 62mm (3.23 × 2.44in)
Maximum speed: 280km/h (175mph); 0 to 97km/h (60mph) 5.6sec
Dimensions: wheelbase 2.52m (8ft 3in); front track 1.5m (4ft 11in); rear track 1.52m (5ft)
Chassis: multi-tubular spaceframes; front suspension independent wishbones, coil springs, dampers and anti-roll bar; rear independent wishbones, coil springs, dampers and anti-roll bar
Brakes: discs front and rear

The Countach continued with engine upgrades in 1985 to 5,167cc, which gave 335kW (455PS) and 0 to 97km/h (60mph) in a very fast 4.8sec. That engine had four valves per cylinder. It was replaced by the Diablo in 1990

Lamborghini Diablo

Country of origin: Italy

Date: introduced in 1991, to replace the Countach

Identity: two-door, two-seat, new hand-built expensive no-holds-barred sports coupé

Engine: mid-mounted longitudinal V12-cylinder dohc; power 356kW (485PS) at 7,000rpm

Gears: five-speed manual only; rear-wheel drive

Capacity: 5.7 litres

Maximum speed: 280km/h (174mph)

Dimensions: wheelbase 2.65m (8ft 8.3in); length 4.46m (14ft 7.6in); width 2.04m (6ft 8.3in); height 1.1m (3ft 7.5in); front track 1.51m (4ft 11.4in); rear track 1.64m (5ft 4.6in)

Chassis: front suspension control arms and coil springs; rear independent control arms and coil springs

Brakes: vented discs front and rear; ABS not available

Kerb weight: 1,655kg (3,640lb)

One of the true exotics at the top of the class, an Italian supercar that demands a long waiting list and an extremely large bank balance, for this is what dreams are made of

Lancia Stratos

Country of origin: Italy
Date: first shown in 1970 at Turin, production lasted from 1972 to 1975, by which time 492 cars had been built
Identity: two-door, two-seat coupé with both roof and tail spoilers designed by Bertone
Engine: 65° V6-cylinder twin ohcs per bank; three Weber carburettors; power 140kW (190PS) at 7,000rpm
Gears: five-speed manual only
Capacity: 2,418cc
Bore and stroke: 92.5 × 60mm (3.64 × 2.36in)
Maximum speed: 209km/h (130mph)
Dimensions: wheelbase 2.18m (7ft 2in); front track 1.43m (4ft 8.5in); rear track 1.46m (4ft 9.5in)
Chassis: monocoque tubular subframes front and rear; front suspension independent wishbones, coil springs, dampers and anti-roll bar; rear independent wishbones, coil springs, dampers and anti-roll bar
Brakes: discs front and rear

Using the Ferrari V6 Dino engine, the Stratos was a highly successful rally car, winning 14 World Championship Rallies and four Monte Carlo Rallies, though it did little to impress on the circuit where it had considerable exposure in Italy

Lotus Elan SE

Country of origin: UK
Date: launched 1988 and available from 1990
Identity: a two-door, two-seat fibreglass-bodied convertible
Engine: front-mounted transverse four-cylinder with alloy head and twin ohc working four valves per cylinder; electronic fuel injection and water-cooled turbocharger; power 123kW (165PS) at 6,600rpm
Gears: five-speed manual only; front-wheel drive
Capacity: 1,588cc
Bore and stroke: 80 × 79mm (3.15 × 3.11in)
Maximum speed: 219km/h (136mph); 0 to 97km/h (60mph) 6.5sec
Dimensions: wheelbase 2.25m (7ft 4.6in); length 3.8m (12ft 5.7in); width 1.73m (5ft 8.3in); height 1.23m (4ft 4.4in)
Chassis: front suspension independent wishbones, coil springs and anti-roll bar; rear independent upper links and wide-based lower wishbones, coil springs and anti-roll bar
Brakes: vented discs front, solid discs rear; ABS not available
Tyres: 205/50 ZR 15
Kerb weight: 1,020kg (2,249lb)

The Elan breaks with Lotus tradition in its front-wheel drive. A super small car, exciting and economical to drive

108

Lotus Esprit Turbo SE

Country of origin: UK
Date: launched at Motorfair 1987
Identity: two-seat two-door coupé; the glass panel across the rear identifies the Turbo model
Engine: mid-mounted longitudinal four-cylinder with alloy head and block, twin ohc working four valves per cylinder; two twin-choke Dellorto carburettors and Garrett T3 turbocharger; power 160kW (212PS) at 6,000rpm
Gears: five-speed manual; rear-wheel drive
Capacity: 2,174cc
Bore and stroke: 95.3 × 76.2mm (3.75 × 3in)
Maximum speed: 241km/h (150mph); 0 to 97km/h (60mph) 5.4sec
Dimensions: wheelbase 2.46m (8ft 0.8in); length 4.33m (14ft 2.5in); width 1.86m (6ft 1.2in); height 1.14m (3ft 8.8in)
Chassis: front suspension independent wishbones and coil springs with coaxial dampers and anti-roll bar; rear independent transverse links with box-section trailing arms, coil springs and coaxial telescopic dampers
Brakes: vented discs front; solid discs rear; ABS standard
Tyres: front 195/60 VR 15; rear 235/60 VR 15
Kerb weight: 1,268kg (2,795lb)

In 1992 the seating space gave 76mm (3in) more headroom and 50mm (2in) more hip-room. Doors open wider, and the deck spoiler is bigger

Maserati Spyder

Country of origin: Italy
Date: production of the biturbo is limited and specifications unchanged since 1990
Identity: two-seat, two-door convertible
Engine: front-mounted longitudinal V6-cylinder ohc; fuel injection; twin iHi exhaust turbos with intercooler; power 165kW (225PS) at 5,600rpm
Gears: four-speed automatic; five-speed manual available; rear-wheel drive
Capacity: 2.8 litres
Maximum speed: 220km/h (137mph)
Dimensions: wheelbase 2.4m (7ft 10.4in); length 4.04m (13ft 3.2in); width 1.71m (5ft 7.4in); height 1.33m (4ft 4.3in); front and rear track 1.42m (4ft 8in)
Chassis: front suspension independent MacPherson struts and coil springs; rear independent semi-trailing arms and coil springs
Brakes: vented discs front; solid discs rear; ABS not available
Kerb weight: 1,333kg (2,934lb)

A high-performance Italian car, with all the appearances of its breeding on show, including the beautiful three-layer Hartz top and a smooth, well-balanced mid-range engine. Maserati is investigating the introduction of a passive restraint system

Mazda 929

Country of origin: Japan
Date: the 1992 Mazda 929 specification is a vast improvement on previous models
Identity: longer, wider and lower, the 929 comes with the novel option of a solar sunroof. A glass panel that collects the sun's energy while the car is parked produces the energy to run the ventilation fan and will also recharge the battery
Engine: front-mounted longitudinal V6-cylinder dohc; 24 valves; electronic fuel injection/ignition; power 143kW (195PS) at 5,750rpm
Gears: four-speed automatic only; rear-wheel drive
Capacity: 3 litres
Maximum speed: 201km/h (125mph)
Dimensions: wheelbase 2.85m (9ft 4.2in); length 4.92m (16ft 1.7in); width 1.79m (5ft 10.7in); height 1.39m (4ft 6.9in)
Chassis: front suspension lower arm wishbones, torsion rod, upper lateral links and leading link, and coil springs; rear independent upper and lower trailing links, hub carrier, triple transverse links and coil springs
Brakes: vented discs front and rear; ABS standard
Kerb weight: 1,634kg (3,596lb)

A luxury sedan with sporting pretensions, ripe for further development

Mazda MX-3 GS

Country of origin: Japan
Date: new for 1992 was the 1.8-litre V6 engine with three spark plugs on each bank
Identity: small two-door 2 + 2 hatchback in the econocoupé class
Engine: front-mounted longitudinal V6-cylinder with two intake and two exhaust valves in each cylinder; power 95kW (130PS) at 6,500rpm
Gears: five-speed manual; four-speed automatic with overdrive available; front-wheel drive
Capacity: 1.8 litres
Maximum speed: 183km/h (114mph)
Dimensions: wheelbase 2.38m (8ft 0.3in); length 4.21m (13ft 9.7in); width 1.69m (5ft 6.7in); height 1.31m (4ft 3.6in)
Chassis: front suspension independent MacPherson struts with sway bar and coil springs; rear independent struts, coil springs, twin trapezoidal links and sway bar
Brakes: vented discs front; solid discs rear; ABS optional
Tyres: 205/55 VR 15
Kerb weight: 1,060kg (2,332lb)

The curvaceous and low frontal area of the MX-3 produces a 0.32 drag coefficient, while inside there are highback bucket seats, a wide hooded instrument panel and a three-spoke steering wheel

Mazda MX-5/Miata

Country of origin: Japan
Date: the specification below is for the 1991 base MX-5; the BBR Turbo is now available
Identity: a two-seat two-door convertible in true fun-motoring style
Engine: front-mounted longitudinal four-cylinder with alloy head and twin ohc working four valves per cylinder; electronic fuel injection; power 85kW (115PS) at 6,500rpm
Gears: five-speed manual only; rear-wheel drive
Capacity: 1,598cc
Bore and stroke: 78 × 84mm (3.07 × 3.31in)
Maximum speed: 183km/h (114mph); 0 to 97km/h (60mph) in 9.1sec
Dimensions: wheelbase 2.26m (7ft 5.2in); length 3.95m (12ft 11.5in); width 1.67m (5ft 5.9in); height 1.23m (4ft 0.2in)
Chassis: front suspension independent wishbones, coil springs and anti-roll bar; rear independent wishbones, coil springs and anti-roll bar
Brakes: vented discs front; solid discs rear; ABS not available
Tyres: 185/60 HR 14
Kerb weight: 990kg (2,185lb)

Very neat, tidy, well-balanced; sporting pop-up headlamps, bumpers integral with bodywork
118 *and a hood which folds easily away*

Mazda MX-6 LS

Country of origin: Japan/USA
Date: the MX-6 has been restyled for 1993, for building in Michigan
Identity: two-door four-seat coupé
Engine: front-mounted longitudinal V6-cylinder dohc; 24 valves; power 120kW (164PS) at 5,600rpm
Gears: four-speed automatic; five-speed manual available; front-wheel drive
Capacity: 2.5 litres
Maximum speed: 201km/h (125mph)
Dimensions: wheelbase 2.61m (8ft 6.8in); length 4.61m (15ft 1.5in); width 1.75m (5ft 8.9in); height 1.31m (4ft 3.6in); front and rear track 1.5m (4ft 11.1in)
Chassis: front suspension independent MacPherson struts, lower control arm and coil springs; rear independent MacPherson struts, twin trapezoidal links and coil springs
Brakes: vented discs front; drums rear; ABS optional
Kerb weight: 1,183kg (2,604lb)

Manufactured at Flat Rock, Michigan, the new MX-6 became available in mid-1992 in just two versions – the standard MX-6 and the more sporty, upscale MX-6 LS, with a newly-designed V6 engine

Mazda RX-7

Country of origin: Japan
Date: completely redesigned for 1992
Identity: two-seat, two-door coupé hatchback or turbocharged cabriolet
Engine: front-mounted longitudinal twin-rotor rotary Wankel engine with diecast housing; fuel injection and Hitachi twin-scroll turbocharger with intercooler; power 147kW (200PS) at 6,500rpm
Gears: five-speed manual; four-speed automatic available; rear-wheel drive
Capacity: chamber capacity 654cc, rated at 2,254cc
Maximum speed: 238km/h (148mph); 0 to 97km/h (60mph) 6.7sec
Dimensions: wheelbase 2.43m (7ft 11.7in), length 4.31m (14ft 1.9in); width 1.69m (5ft 6.5in); height 1.26m (4ft 1.8in)
Chassis: front suspension independent MacPherson struts and anti-roll bar; rear independent semi-trailing arms, multi-link layout with coil springs and anti-roll bar
Brakes: vented discs front and rear; ABS standard
Tyres: 205/55 ZR 16
Kerb weight: 1,330kg (2,933lb)

The refined 13B rotary engine is at the heart of this much-improved RX-7, handling excellently with fully-independent suspension

122

Mercedes-Benz 300 SL

Country of origin: Germany
Date: the 500 SL first appeared in 1982
Identity: a very well-equipped two-door roadster has most of the 500 SL safety features
Engine: front-mounted longitudinal six-cylinder with alloy head and block and twin ohc, working four valves per cylinder; Bosch KE5 CIS fuel injection; power 170kW (231PS) at 6,300rpm
Gears: five-speed automatic standard; rear-wheel drive
Capacity: 2,960cc
Bore and stroke: 89 × 80mm (3.5 × 3.15in)
Maximum speed: 216km/h (134mph); 0 to 97km/h (60mph) 8.6sec
Dimensions: wheelbase 2.51m (8ft 3in); length 4.47m (14ft 7.9in); width 1.81m (5ft 11.3in); height 1.3m (4ft 3.2in)
Chassis: front suspension independent MacPherson struts and anti-roll bar; rear independent five-link location with coil springs and anti-roll bar, anti-squat and anti-drive control
Brakes: vented discs front, solid discs rear
Tyres: 225/55 ZR 16
Kerb weight: 1,690kg (3,725lb)

A superb car, with the unusual feature of a five-speed automatic transmission which also has a mode control switch offering Economy (E) or Sport (S)

Mercedes-Benz S-class

Country of origin: Germany
Date: introduced at Geneva in 1991
Identity: every item of luxury in this top-of-the-class roadster included here
Engine: front-mounted longitudinal V12-cylinder with alloy block and heads; twin ohc per bank working four valves per cylinder, varying intake valve timing; advanced ignition/injection control system; power 300kW (408PS) at 5,200rpm
Gears: four-speed automatic standard; rear-wheel drive
Capacity: 5,987cc
Bore and stroke: 89 × 80.2mm (3.5 × 3.16in)
Maximum speed: 250km/h (155mph); 0 to 100km/h (62mph) 6sec
Dimensions: wheelbase 3.04m (9ft 11.7in); length 5.11m (16ft 9.3in); width 1.88m (6ft 2.3in); height 1.49m (4ft 10.7in)
Chassis: front suspension independent wishbones and coil springs, with anti-drive control, gas-filled dampers and anti-roll bar; rear independent multi-link layout with coil springs and gas-filled dampers, anti-squat and anti-lift control with self-levelling, anti-roll bar
Brakes: vented discs front and rear
Tyres: 235/60 ZR 16
Kerb weight: 2,180kg (4,806lb)

Top of the range 600 SE (SEL long
wheelbase)

Mercury Capri

Country of origin: USA
Date: 1992 specification for the high-performance model XR2
Identity: two-door 2 + 2 convertible
Engine: front-mounted longitudinal dohc; turbocharger with intercooler; power 97kW (132PS) at 6,000rpm
Gears: five-speed manual only, with overdrive fourth; front-wheel drive
Capacity: 1.6 litres
Maximum speed: 195km/h (121mph)
Dimensions: wheelbase 2.4m (7ft 10.7in) length 4.22m (13ft 10.1in); width 1.64m (5ft 4.6in); height 1.32m (4ft 4.2in)
Chassis: front suspension independent struts and coil springs; rear independent struts, twin trapezoidal links and coil springs
Brakes: vented discs front; solid discs rear; ABS not available
Tyres: 195/50 VR 15
Kerb weight: 1,092kg (2,404lb)

Good seats, improved tyres, power rack and pinion steering, tinted glass and power windows are now standard, along with alloy wheels and tighter suspension; a hardtop conversion is available

Mitsubishi 3000 GT

Country of origin: Japan
Date: a relatively new car on the streets; the specification below is for the 1992 model, which remains basically unaltered since its introduction
Identity: a two-door, 2 + 2 coupé also available in base and mid-range SL versions
Engine: front-mounted longitudinal V6-cylinder dohc; twin turbocharger with inter-cooler; power 220kW (300PS) at 6,000rpm
Gears: five-speed manual; four-speed automatic available; four-wheel drive
Capacity: 3 litres
Maximum speed: 238km/h (148mph)
Dimensions: wheelbase 2.47m (8ft 1.2in); length 4.58m (15ft 0.5in); width 1.84m (6ft 0.4in); height 1.25m (4ft 1.1in)
Chassis: front suspension independent Mac-Pherson struts and coil springs; rear independent double wishbones, dual links, trailing arms and coil springs
Brakes: vented discs front; solid discs rear; ABS standard
Tyres: 225/50 ZR 17
Kerb weight: 1,398kg (3,076lb)

With four-wheel steering and electrically-controlled suspension, the 3000 GT packs a lot of power into a well-equipped coupé

Mitsubishi Diamante

Country of origin: Japan
Date: a replacement for the Acura Legend; the 1992 specification below is for the LS model
Identity: a luxury-oriented two-door sports sedan
Engine: front-mounted longitudinal V6-cylinder 18-valve dohc; power 148kW (202PS) at 6,000rpm
Gears: four-speed automatic only; front-wheel drive
Capacity: 3 litres
Maximum speed: 230 km/h (143mph); 0 to 100km/h (62mph) 8.1sec
Dimensions: wheelbase 2.72m (8ft 11.1in); length 4.83m (15ft 10.2in); width 1.77m (5ft 9.9in); height 1.41m (4ft 7.5in)
Chassis: front suspension independent Mac-Pherson struts and offset coil springs; rear independent trailing arms with assist links and coil springs
Brakes: vented discs front and rear; ABS standard
Tyres: 225/50 VR 16
Kerb weight: 1,558kg (3,428lb)

Based on a stretched 3,000 GT platform and suspension components, the Diamante includes a wide range of electrical devices, including an optional Euro Handling package

Mitsubishi Eclipse GSX

Country of origin: Japan
Date: a better-looking car for 1992, but mechanically unchanged from previous years
Identity: two-door 2 + 2 coupé; also available in base, GS, GS DOHC 16 and GS DOHC 16 turbo versions
Engine: front-mounted longitudinal four-cylinder with ohc; electronic ignition/injection, turbocharger with intercooler; power 132kW (180PS) at 6,000rpm
Gears: five-speed manual; four-speed automatic available; four-wheel drive
Capacity: 2 litres
Maximum speed: 225km/h (140mph); 0 to 97km/h (60mph) 7.2sec
Dimensions: wheelbase 2.47m (8ft 1.2in); length 4.39m (14ft 4.8in); width 1.69m (5ft 6.7in); height 1.3m (4ft 3.4in)
Chassis: front suspension independent MacPherson struts, control arms, coil springs and anti-roll bar; rear independent double wishbones, toe control and anti-roll bar
Brakes: vented discs front; solid discs rear; ABS optional
Tyres: 195/60 VR 15
Kerb weight: 1,147kg (2,524lb)

The Eclipse uses Galant parts on a shorter wheelbase, power-assisted four-wheel disc brakes and tilt steering wheel

134

Mitsubishi Galant

Country of origin: Japan
Date: 1989 as Galant saloon; coupé in 1990
Identity: attractive four-wheel drive, four-wheel steering coupé
Engine: front-mounted transverse four-cylinder with alloy head and twin ohc working four valves per cylinder; electronic multi-point fuel injection; power 110 kW (150PS) at 6,750rpm
Gears: five-speed manual; automatic available; four-wheel drive
Capacity: 1,997cc
Bore and stroke: 85 × 88mm (3.34 × 3.46in)
Maximum speed: 190km/h (118mph); 0 to 97km/h (60mph) 9.4sec
Dimensions: wheelbase 2.6m (8ft 6.4in); length 4.57m (15ft); width 1.695m (5ft 6.7in); height 1.41m (4ft 7.5in)
Chassis: front suspension independent MacPherson struts and anti-roll bar; rear independent wishbones, trailing arms, concentric coil springs and anti-roll bar
Brakes: vented discs front; solid discs rear; ABS standard
Tyres: 195/60 R 15 87V
Kerb weight: 1,340kg (2,954lb)

The four-wheel drive is permanently engaged, with the rear wheels turning in the same direction as the front ones, returning to straight-ahead below 50km/h (31mph)

Nissan 100 NX Sunny

Country of origin: Japan
Date: new Sunny range introduced in 1991
Identity: small two-door, 2 + 2 coupé
Engine: front-mounted transverse four-cylinder with alloy block and twin ohc working four valves per cylinder; single-point fuel injection; power 70kW (95PS) at 6,000rpm
Gears: five-speed manual; automatic available; front-wheel drive
Capacity: 1,597cc
Bore and stroke: 76 × 88mm (3 × 3.46in)
Maximum speed: 180km/h (112mph); 0 to 100km/h (62mph) 10.8sec
Dimensions: wheelbase 2.43m (7ft 11.7in); length 4.13m (13ft 6.8in); width 1.67m (5ft 5.7in); height 1.31m (4ft 3.6in)
Chassis: front suspension independent Mac-Pherson struts; rear independent parallel links
Brakes: vented discs front; drums rear; ABS not available
Tyres: 155 SR 13
Kerb weight: 940kg (2,072lb)

Sporty in appearance, the 100 NX has wrap-around seats, a T-bar roof and headlamps set into deep scoops

Nissan 200 SX

Country of origin: Japan
Date: launched at Birmingham in 1988; available in 1989
Identity: a stylish 2 + 2 sports coupé, it replaces the Silvia Turbo 1.82 ZX
Engine: front-mounted longitudinal four-cylinder with ohc working four valves per cylinder; electronic ignition/injection and turbocharger; power 126kW (171PS) at 6,400rpm
Gears: five-speed manual; five-speed automatic available; rear-wheel drive
Capacity: 1,809cc
Bore and stroke: 83 × 83.6mm (3.27 × 3.29in)
Maximum speed: 225km/h (140mph); 0 to 97km/h (60mph) 7.2sec
Dimensions: wheelbase 2.47m (8ft 1.4in); length 4.53m (14ft 10.5in); width 1.69m (5ft 6.5in); height 1.29m (4ft 2.8in)
Chassis: front suspension independent MacPherson struts and anti-roll bar; rear independent multi-link location, coil springs and anti-roll bar
Brakes: vented discs front; solid discs rear; ABS standard
Tyres: 195/60 VR 15
Kerb weight: 1,190kg (2,623lb)

An exciting nippy car, easy to handle, it performs well; front bumpers are colour keyed, headlamps are pop-up

Nissan 300 ZX

Country of origin: Japan
Date: launched in 1989; available from 1990
Identity: smoothly styled 2 + 2 sports coupé
Engine: front-mounted longitudinal V6-cylinder with alloy heads and twin ohc per bank working four valves per cylinder; electronic fuel injection; twin turbochargers; power 205kW (208PS) at 6,400rpm
Gears: five-speed manual with five-speed automatic available; rear-wheel drive
Capacity: 2,960cc
Bore and stroke: 87 × 83mm (3.42 × 3.27in)
Maximum speed: 230km/h (143mph); 0 to 97km/h (60mph) 7sec
Dimensions: wheelbase 2.57m (8ft 5.2in); length 2.57m (14ft 10in); width 1.8m (5ft 10.9in); height 1.25m (4ft 1.4in)
Chassis: front suspension independent multi-link wheel location, coil springs and anti-roll bar; rear independent multi-link location, coil springs and anti-roll bar
Brakes: vented discs front and rear; ABS standard
Tyres: front 225/50 ZR 16; rear 245/45 ZR 16
Kerb weight: 1,585kg (3,494lb)

The 300 ZX incorporates a four-wheel computer-controlled steering system offering greater high-speed stability and a double-cone synchromesh gearbox

142

Oldmobile Achieva SC

Country of origin: USA
Date: launched in early 1992
Identity: available in a range to include S and SL coupés and the more powerful SC and SCX two-door coupés
Engine: front-mounted longitudinal V6-cylinder ohv; power 117kW (160PS) at 5,200rpm
Gears: five-speed manual; three-speed automatic available; front-wheel drive
Capacity: 3.3 litres
Maximum speed: 187km/h (116mph); 0 to 97km/h (60mph) 8.9sec
Dimensions: wheelbase 2.62m (8ft 7.4in); length 4.77m (15ft 7.9in); width 1.7m (5ft 7.2in); height 1.35m (4ft 5.1in)
Chassis: front suspension independent Mac-Pherson struts and coil springs; rear beam axle, trailing arms, coil springs and shock absorbers
Brakes: vented discs front; drums rear; ABS standard
Tyres: P215/65 R 15
Kerb weight: 1,222kg (2,690lb)

This roomy coupé can seat five. Flush-mounted glass, wet-arm windshield wipers and rear-seat heat ducts all add to the luxury, together with the optional variable-effect power steering

Plymouth Laser RS Turbo

Country of origin: USA
Date: integrated headlamps and the turbocharged engine were introduced for the 1982 models
Identity: two-door 2 + 2 sports coupé available in base, RS and RS Turbo models
Engine: front-mounted longitudinal 16-valve dohc; turbocharger with intercooler; power 143kW (195PS) at 6,000rpm
Gears: five-speed manual; four-speed automatic available; four-wheel drive
Capacity: 2 litres
Maximum speed: 206km/h (128mph); 0 to 97km/h (60mph) 6.4sec
Dimensions: wheelbase 2.47m (8ft 1.2in); length 4.39m (14ft 4.8in); width 1.69m (5ft 6.7in); height 1.3m (4ft 3.4in); front and rear track 1.46m (4ft 9.7in)
Chassis: front suspension independent MacPherson struts and coil springs; rear independent double wishbone and coil springs
Brakes: vented discs front; solid discs rear; ABS optional
Kerb weight: 1,147kg (2,524lb)

The Laser now offers exciting runabout motoring with a host of standard equipment. The well balanced 2-litre engine with turbo attached, rack and pinion steering and all-wheel drive should prove successful for Plymouth

146

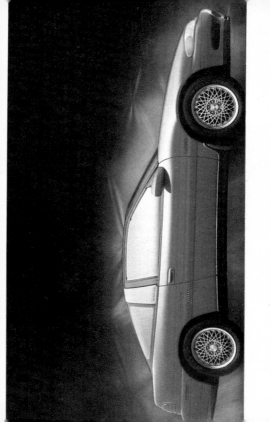

Pontiac Bonneville SSEi

Country of origin: USA
Date: major alterations are incorporated in the 1992 specification throughout the range
Identity: base model with W21 sports package, including 16-inch wheels and F41 suspension
Engine: front-mounted longitudinal V6-cylinder supercharged; electronic ignition/injection; power 150kW (205PS) at 4,400rpm
Gears: four-speed automatic only; front-wheel drive
Capacity: 3.8 litres
Maximum speed: 190km/h (118mph)
Dimensions: wheelbase 2.81m (9ft 2.8in); length 5.09m (16ft 8.6in); width 1.87m (6ft 1.6in); height 1.41m (4ft 7.5in)
Chassis: front suspension independent MacPherson struts and coil springs; rear semi-independent MacPherson struts, beam axle, trailing arms and coil springs
Brakes: vented discs front; drums rear; ABS standard
Tyres: 225/60 R 16 Eagle GT
Kerb weight: 1,528kg (3,362lb)

The large-bodied Bonneville is available in models from a four-door five-passenger sedan through to the more powerful sporting SSEi, with well-equipped sports package. A rear spoiler is optional, as is traction control

Pontiac Fiero

Country of origin: USA
Date: production started 1979, ended 1988
Identity: stylish wedge-shaped two-door two-seat sports coupé
Engine: rear-mounted transverse V6-cylinder with pushrod overhead-valve design; power 103kW (140PS)
Gears: five-speed manual; rear-wheel drive
Capacity: 2,836cc
Maximum speed: 180km/h (112mph)
Dimensions: wheelbase 2.2m (7ft 2.5in); track 1.35m (4ft 5in)
Chassis: front suspension independent MacPherson struts, coil springs and anti-roll bar; rear independent MacPherson struts, lower wishbone, single links and anti-roll bar
Brakes: solid discs front and rear
Tyres: 185/60 HR 14
Kerb weight: 1,045kg (2,300lb)

Although the spaceframe with unstressed plastic body panels was advanced, the Fiero consisted of too many components from other cars, and although upgraded with the larger 2,836cc engine in 1987, together with the five-speed gearbox and fastback body style, a series of engine fires prompted a massive recall from which the Fiero has never recovered

150

Pontiac Firebird Trans Am

Country of origin: USA
Date: by the late 1970s, stringent USA emission controls meant engine alterations for the Firebird, for which the 1979 specification is detailed below
Identity: two-door 2 + 2 convertible
Engine: front-mounted at 90° V8-cylinder; Rochester carburettor; Garrett AiResearch turbocharger; power 150kW (205PS) at 4,000rpm
Gears: three-speed automatic; rear-wheel drive
Capacity: 4,940cc
Bore and stroke: 101.6 × 76.2mm (4 × 3in)
Maximum speed: 170km/h (110mph)
Dimensions: wheelbase 2.74m (9ft); front track 1.55m (5ft 1in); rear track 1.52m (5ft)
Chassis: front suspension independent wishbones with lower trailing links, coil springs, dampers and anti-roll bar; rear rigid axle, semi-elliptical leaf springs, dampers and anti-roll bar
Brakes: vented discs front and rear

The 1979 model also had several new features such as spoilers made of more flexible and durable material and was available in a wider range of colours. Out of 211,454 Firebirds produced in 1979, over half were Trans Am models

Pontiac Firebird Trans Am convertible

Country of origin: USA
Date: 1992 model specification
Identity: two-door 2 + 2 hatchback or convertible
Engine: front-mounted longitudinal V8-cylinder; power 176kW (240PS) at 4,400rpm
Gears: five-speed manual; four-speed automatic available; rear-wheel drive
Capacity: 5.7 litres
Maximum speed: 232km/h (144mph)
Dimensions: wheelbase 2.56m (8ft 5in); length 4.95m (16ft 3.1in); width 1.84m (6ft 0.4in); height 1.26m (4ft 1.7in)
Chassis: front suspension independent MacPherson struts, coil springs and anti-roll bar; rear independent live axle, lateral links, torque arm, coil springs and anti-roll bar
Brakes: vented discs front and rear; ABS not available
Tyres: 215/60 VR 16
Kerb weight: 1,418kg (3,121lb)

The Trans Am now has swoopier body parts and the F41 suspension, a limited-slip differential plus a quieter, better-fitting interior and

154 *asbestos-free brake pads*

Pontiac Formula Firehawk

Country of origin: USA
Date: 1992 specification
Identity: two-door, four-seater street-legal race-car
Engine: front-mounted, longitudinal V8-cylinder ohv with two valves per cylinder and aluminium heads; power 257kW (350PS) at 5,500rpm
Gears: six-speed manual only; rear-wheel drive
Capacity: 5,733cc
Maximum speed: 250km/h (155mph); 0 to 97km/h (60mph) 4.9sec
Dimensions: wheelbase 2.56m (8ft 5in); length 4.95m (16ft 3.1in)
Chassis: front suspension independent MacPherson struts and coil springs; rear Dana 44 limited-slip live axle with torque arm, coil springs, lower control arms, track bar and anti-roll bar
Brakes: vented discs front and rear
Tyres: 275/40 ZR 17 Firestone Firehawk
Kerb weight: 1,545kg (3,400lb)

Plenty of power and good cornering adhesion, built to be competitive in the IMSA Bridgestone Potenza Supercar 'showroom stock' racing series; a no-holds-barred race-car for the street. The interior is unchanged and production is set to run to 250 units only

Pontiac Grand Am

Country of origin: USA
Date: redesigned for 1992
Identity: two-door GT coupé; four-door sedan also available
Engine: front-mounted longitudinal V6-cylinder ohv; electronic ignition/injection; power 117kW (160PS) at 5,200rpm
Gears: five-speed manual; three-speed automatic available; front-wheel drive
Capacity: 3.3 litres
Maximum speed: 220km/h (137mph)
Dimensions: wheelbase 2.62m (8ft 7.4in); length 4.75m (15ft 6.9in); width 1.74m (5ft 8.6in); height 1.35m (4ft 5.1in); front track 1.41m (4ft 7.6in); rear track 1.4m (4ft 7.2in)
Chassis: front suspension independent MacPherson struts, coil springs and anti-roll bar; rear beam axle, tube shock absorbers and coil springs
Brakes: vented discs front; drums rear; ABS standard
Tyres: 205/55 VR 15
Kerb weight: 1,240kg (2,728lb)

Externally altered, the new GT coupé also includes redesigned front brakes as well as the GM-developed ABS VI. The inside is roomier and the ergonomics more user-friendly

Pontiac Grand Prix

Country of origin: USA
Date: launched in the summer of 1987
Identity: two-door coupé (GTP), smoother in line than the Grand Am although slightly larger and more powerful
Engine: front-mounted longitudinal V6-cylinder dual cam; electronic ignition/injection power 154kW (210PS) at 5,200rpm
Gears: four-speed automatic with a second-gear start-up switch for use in slippery traction situations; five-speed manual available; front-wheel drive
Capacity: 3.4 litres
Maximum speed: 222km/h (138mph)
Dimensions: wheelbase 2.73m (8ft 11.5in) length 4.95m (16ft 2.8in); width 1.82m (5ft 11.9in); height 1.35m (4ft 5.3in)
Chassis: front suspension independent struts, control arms and coil springs; rear independent struts, trailing link, lateral links and transverse leaf springs
Brakes: vented discs front; solid discs rear; ABS standard
Tyres: 215/60 XR 15
Kerb weight: 1,461kg (3,214lb)

Now with independent suspension, four-wheel disc brakes and power rack and pinion steering, the Grand Prix gets more comfortable by the year

Porsche 911 Carrera RS

Country of origin: Germany
Date: launched in 1990, available in mid-1991
Identity: 10 per cent lighter with 10 per cent more power than the standard model, the RS has a rear spoiler which rises automatically at 80.5km/h (50mph)
Engine: rear-mounted longitudinal flat six-cylinder with air cooling and dry sump lubrication; Bosch Motronics and twin ignition system; power 191kW (260PS) at 6,100rpm
Gears: five-speed manual; rear-wheel drive
Capacity: 3,600cc
Bore and stroke: 100 × 76.4mm (3.94 × 3in)
Maximum speed: 261km/h (162mph); 0 to 100km/h (62mph) 5.4sec
Dimensions: wheelbase 2.27m (7ft 5.5in); length 4.29m (14ft 0.9in); width 1.65m (5ft 5in); height 1.31m (4ft 3.6in)
Chassis: front suspension independent struts with torsion bars and anti-roll bar; rear independent semi-trailing arms and torsion bars and anti-roll bar
Brakes: vented and cross-drilled discs front and rear; ABS standard
Tyres: front 205/50 ZR 17; rear 255/40 ZR 17
Kerb weight: 1,250kg (2,755lb)

The front bonnet is in aluminium, the ride height 40mm lower and the whole tuned for a higher performance

162

Porsche 911 Carrera 2/4 Turbo

Country of origin: Germany
Date: the standard model 911 originally appeared in 1964, and the Turbo in 1975; below is the 1992 specification
Identity: two-door 2+2 coupé with wrap-around polymer bumpers, modestly flared wheel wells, a smooth underbelly and the famous whale-tail parachute
Engine: rear-mounted longitudinal flat six-cylinder ohc; turbocharger with intercooler power 181kW (247PS) at 6,100rpm
Gears: five-speed manual; four-speed automatic available; rear-wheel drive
Capacity: 3,299cc
Maximum speed: 257km/h (160mph)
Dimensions: wheelbase 2.27m (7ft 5.4in); length 4.25m (13ft 11.3in); width 1.65m (5ft 5in); height 1.32m (4ft 4in)
Chassis: front suspension independent strut located by control arm, coil springs and anti-roll bar; rear independent semi-trailing arm and coil springs
Brakes: vented discs front and rear
Tyres: front 205/50 ZR 17; rear 255/40 ZR 17
Kerb weight: 1,377kg (3,031lb)

The Carrera is now supplied with force-sensitive power steering, anti-lock brakes and dual airbags

Porsche 924 Carrera GTS

Country of origin: Germany
Date: first shown at the Frankfurt Motor Show in 1979; the Carrera GT production model was available in 1980, and the GTS the following year
Identity: coupé-bodied 2 + 2 with extended wheel arches and front and rear spoilers
Engine: Audi four-stroke four-cylinder ohv, single ohc; electronic Bosch K Jetronic fuel injection; KKK turbocharger with intercooler; power 180kW (245PS) at 6,250rpm
Gears: five-speed manual; rear-wheel drive
Capacity: 1,984cc
Bore and stroke: 86.5 × 84.4mm (3.4 × 3.32in)
Maximum speed: 225km/h (140mph)
Dimensions: wheelbase 2.4m (7ft 10.5in); length 4.21m (13ft 9.7in); width 1.68m (5ft 6.3in); height 1.27m (4ft 2in)
Chassis: front suspension independent Mac-Pherson struts, lower wishbones, coil springs, telescopic dampers and anti-roll bar; rear independent semi-trailing arms, transverse torsion bars, coil springs, telescopic dampers and anti-roll bar
Brakes: vented discs front and rear
Tyres: front 205/55VR; rear 225/50 VR 16
Kerb weight: 1,080kg (2,376lb)

The 924 was the first front-engined water-cooled Porsche to take part in the Le Mans 24-Hour Race, in 1980

Porsche 928 GT

Country of origin: Germany
Date: originating 1977, GT introduced 1989
Identity: rounded tail and alloy wheels
Engine: front-mounted longitudinal V8-cylinder with all-alloy construction, chain and toothed belt drive to twin ohc, each bank working four valves per cylinder; Bosch Jetronic injection; power 243kW (330PS) at 6,200rpm
Gears: five-speed manual, automatic available; rear-wheel drive
Capacity: 4,957cc
Bore and stroke: 100 × 78.9mm (3.94 × 3.1in)
Maximum speed: 266km/h (165mph); 0 to 97km/h (60mph) 5.6sec
Dimensions: wheelbase 2.5m (8ft 2.4in); length 4.52m (14ft 10in); width 1.83m (6ft 0.8in); height 1.28m (4ft 2.5in)
Chassis: front suspension independent wishbones and coil springs and anti-roll bar; rear independent semi-trailing arms and upper transverse links, coil springs with self-levelling provision and anti-roll bar
Brakes: vented discs front and rear
Tyres: front 225/50 VR 16; rear 245/45 ZR 16
Kerb weight: 1,580kg (3,484lb)

The technical brilliance of the 928 so overwhelmed European motoring journalists that they voted it Car of the Year in 1977; the first time for a purely sports car

168

Porsche 944

Country of origin: Germany
Date: originally in 1981 the 944 had a 2.5 litre
engine, which has now been increased to 3 litres
Identity: available as either a coupé with round-
ed rear window or cabriolet with an electric hood
Engine: front-mounted longitudinal four-
cylinder with all-alloy construction, belt-driven
twin ohc working four valves per cylinder; Bosch
Motronics; power 155kW (211PS) at 5,800rpm
Gears: five-speed manual only; rear-wheel drive
Capacity: 2,990cc
Bore and stroke: 104 × 88mm (4.09 × 3.46in)
Maximum speed: 235km/h (146mph); 0 to
97km/h (60mph) 6sec
Dimensions: wheelbase 2.4m (7ft 10.5in);
length 4.2m (13ft 9.3in); width 1.73m (5ft 8.3in);
height 1.27m (4ft 2.2in)
Chassis: front suspension independent Mac-
Pherson struts and anti-roll bar; rear independent
semi-trailing arms and torsion bars, anti-roll bar
Brakes: vented discs front and rear; ABS
standard
Tyres: front 205/55 ZR 16; rear 225/50 ZR 16
Kerb weight: 1,340kg (2,955lb)

*Both fog lamps and headlamps are
mounted in the impact-absorbing
nose section and the gearbox is rear-
mounted in a transaxle*

Porsche 968

Country of origin: Germany
Date: first shown in 1986, the 968 has now come of age
Identity: two-door 2 + 2 coupé or convertible
Engine: front-mounted longitudinal inline 4-dohc, four valves per cylinder, with Variocam electric/hydraulic valve timing
Gears: six-speed manual; four-speed Tiptronic automatic available; rear-wheel drive
Capacity: 2,990cc
Maximum speed: 235km/h (146mph)
Dimensions: wheelbase 2.4m (7ft 10.5in); length 4.32m (14ft 2.1in); width 1.73m (5ft 8.3in); height 1.27m (4ft 2.2in)
Chassis: front suspension independent Mac-Pherson struts, control arms and coil springs; rear independent trailing arms, torsion bars and anti-roll bar
Brakes: vented discs front and rear; ABS standard
Tyres: front 225/45 ZR 17; rear 255/40 ZR 17
Kerb weight: 1,403kg (3,086lb)

Starting with the 944 model, Porsche decreased the weight and then carried out extensive bodywork modifications, utilising some of the 911 and 959 styling to produce a better-handling and better-driving car than the previous

172 *model*

Saturn Sports

Country of origin: USA
Date: still making slow development improvements, the 1992 model has reduced engine noise
Identity: four-passenger 2 + 2 coupé (SC), also available as a sedan (SL)
Engine: front-mounted longitudinal four-cylinder twin-cam; power 91kW (124PS) at 6,000rpm
Gears: five-speed manual; four-speed automatic available; front-wheel drive
Capacity: 1.9 litres
Maximum speed: 185km/h (115mph)
Dimensions: wheelbase 2.6m (8ft 6.4in); length 4.48m (14ft 8.3in); width 1.71m (5ft 7.6in); height 1.28m (4ft 2.6in)
Chassis: front suspension MacPherson struts and coil springs; rear independent Tri-link struts and coil springs
Brakes: vented discs front; drums rear; ABS optional
Tyres: 185/60 HR 14
Kerb weight: 1,085kg (2,388lb)

A basic budget-priced sports coupé, still in need of further refinements to both engine and equipment. Bright finish teardrop wheels and decklid spoilers are optional extras

Subaru SVX

Country of origin: Japan/USA
Date: the specification which follows was upgraded for 1992
Identity: a new Giugiaro-styled two-door 2 + 2 arrival to the luxury sports coupé market
Engine: front-mounted longitudinal flat six-cylinder 24-valve dohc; power 169kW (230PS) at 5,400rpm
Gears: four-speed automatic with overdrive only; four-wheel drive
Capacity: 3.3 litres
Maximum speed: 225km/h (140mph); 0 to 97km/h (60mph) 7.2sec
Dimensions: wheelbase 2.61m (8ft 6.8in); length 4.62m (15ft 2.1in); width 1.77m (5ft 9.7in); height 1.3m (4ft 3.2in)
Chassis: front suspension MacPherson struts, lower control arm and coil springs; rear fully independent MacPherson struts, twin parallel links and coil springs
Brakes: vented discs front; solid discs rear; ABS standard
Tyres: 225/50 VR 16 Bridgestone
Kerb weight: 1,602kg (3,535lb)

No shortage of electronic extras here; power sunroof and motorised seatbelt are included, and go to
176 *complement the excellent ride*

Toyota Celica GT4

Country of origin: Japan
Date: launched in November 1989, this is the fifth generation of Celica models
Identity: a good-looking, sleek and well-equipped car with pop-up headlamps
Engine: front-mounted transverse four-cylinder with alloy head and twin ohc, working four valves per cylinder; electronic injection and turbocharger with air-air intercooler; power 150kW (204PS) at 6,000rpm
Gears: five-speed manual only; four-wheel drive
Capacity: 1,998cc
Bore and stroke: 86 × 86mm (3.38 × 3.38in)
Maximum speed: 212km/h (132mph); 0 to 97km/h (60mph) 8.1sec
Dimensions: wheelbase 2.52m (8ft 3.4in); length 4.43m (14ft 6.4in); width 1.74m (5ft 8.7in); height 1.3m (4ft 3.2in)
Chassis: front suspension independent MacPherson struts and anti-roll bar; rear independent MacPherson struts and anti-roll bar
Brakes: vented discs front; solid discs rear; ABS standard
Tyres: 215/50 VR 15
Kerb weight: 1,890kg (4,166lb)

A well-equipped car, with a better and stronger body than before, owing to use of galvanealed steel

Toyota MR-2

Country of origin: Japan
Date: the current version was launched in 1990
Identity: small mid-engined sports GT
Engine: mid-mounted transverse four-cylinder with twin ohc working four valves per cylinder and varying induction by altering lift and opening times of valves; electronic injection; power 118kW (160PS) at 6,000rpm
Gears: five-speed manual only, automatic available on standard model; rear-wheel drive
Capacity: 1,998cc
Bore and stroke: 86 × 86mm (3.38 × 3.38in)
Maximum speed: 220km/h (137mph); 0 to 97km/h (60mph) 6.7sec
Dimensions: wheelbase 2.4m (7ft 10.5in); length 4.18m (13ft 8.6in); width 1.7m (5ft 6.9in); height 1.24m (4ft 0.8in)
Chassis: front suspension independent MacPherson struts and anti-roll bar; rear independent MacPherson struts and anti-roll bar
Brakes: vented discs front and rear; ABS not available
Tyres: front 195/60 R 14 85V; rear 205/60 R 14 88V
Kerb weight: 1,275kg (2,810lb)

The T-bar has removable glass roof panels, but although the inside is a little cramped, this just adds to the exciting drive; leather upholstery is standard

180

Toyota Paseo

Country of origin: Japan
Date: new for the 1990s, the Paseo has yet to make its mark, but its budget price and improvements to come should see it established in a few years
Identity: two door 2 + 2 coupé
Engine: front-mounted longitudinal four-cylinder dohc; 16 valves; power 73kW (100PS) at 6,400rpm
Gears: five-speed manual; four-speed automatic available; front-wheel drive
Capacity: 1.5 litres
Maximum speed: 201km/h (125mph)
Dimensions: wheelbase 2.38m (7ft 9.7in); length 4.14m (13ft 7.2in); width 1.65m (5ft 5.2in); height 1.27m (4ft 2.2in); front track 1.4m (4ft 7.3in); rear track 1.39m (4ft 6.9in)
Chassis: front suspension independent Mac-Pherson struts, trailing torsion bar and coil springs; rear MacPherson struts and coil springs
Brakes: vented discs front; drums rear; ABS not available
Tyres: 195/60 HR 14
Kerb weight: 941kg (2,070lb)

A derivative of the established Tercel with upgraded systems packed into a 2 + 2 coupé, still in need of some refinements which are promised for the future, to include
ABS and airbags

Toyota Supra Turbo

Country of origin: Japan
Date: the all-new Supra was launched in 1986, and this turbocharged model added in 1989
Identity: a fast two-door 2 + 2 coupé with flat deck front and removable roof panels
Engine: front-mounted longitudinal six-cylinder with all-alloy construction and belt-driven ohc working four valves per cylinder; multi-point fuel injection; turbocharger and intercooler; power 173kW (232PS) at 5,600rpm
Gears: five-speed manual or automatic available; rear-wheel drive
Capacity: 2,954cc
Bore and stroke: 83 × 91mm (3.27 × 3.58in)
Maximum speed: 232km/h (144mph); 0 to 97km/h (60mph) 6.9sec
Dimensions: wheelbase 2.6m (8ft 6.4in); length 4.62m (15ft 1.9in); width 1.74m (5ft 8.7in); height 1.31m (4ft 3.6in)
Chassis: front suspension independent wishbones and coil springs and anti-roll bar; rear independent wishbones and coil springs and anti-roll bar
Brakes: vented discs front and rear; ABS standard
Tyres: 225/50 VR 16
Kerb weight: 1,575kg (3,470lb)

A well-equipped fast sports car with an uprated model with a dohc 3.8-litre inline-six engine expected

TVR Griffith

Country of origin: UK
Date: launched at Birmingham in 1990
Identity: a high-speed lightweight two-door, two-seat convertible
Engine: front-mounted, longitudinal V8-cylinder with alloy block and heads; pushrod ohv; electronic fuel injection; power 177kW (240PS) at 6,250rpm
Gears: five-speed manual only; rear-wheel drive
Capacity: 3,947cc
Bore and stroke: 94 × 71.1mm (3.7 × 2.8in)
Maximum speed: 238km/h (148mph); 0 to 97km/h (60mph) 4.9sec
Dimensions: wheelbase 2.3m (7ft 6.6in); length 3.88m (12ft 8.8in); width 1.70m (5ft 7in); height 1.17m (3ft 10.1in)
Chassis: front suspension independent wishbones and coil springs and anti-roll bar; rear independent semi-trailing arms, coil springs and anti-roll bar
Brakes: vented discs front; solid discs rear; ABS not available
Tyres: 215/60 XR 15
Kerb weight: 950kg (2,095lb)

Evolved in conjunction with the TVR racing programme, the Griffith sports electric windows, folding rear quarter hood and removable targa roof panel

TVR S3C

Country of origin: UK
Date: first launched in 1986 as the S, the S3C was shown at Birmingham in 1990
Identity: traditional 1960s styling reintroduced by TVR for this sporting two-seater
Engine: front-mounted longitudinal V6-cylinder Ford engine with three-way catalyst, low pressure drop exhaust system, cast-iron block and heads; pushrod ohv; Bosch L-Jetronic fuel injection; power 125kW (170PS) at 6,000rpm
Gears: five-speed manual only; rear-wheel drive
Capacity: 2,933cc
Bore and stroke: 93 × 72mm (3.66 × 2.83in)
Maximum speed: 206km/h (128mph); 0 to 97km/h (60mph) 7.6sec
Dimensions: wheelbase 2.28m (7ft 6in), length 3.96m (12ft 11.8in); width 1.66m (5ft 5.6in); height 1.22m (4ft 0.1in)
Chassis: fibreglass body on tubular steel chassis; front suspension independent wishbones, coil springs and anti-roll bar; rear independent semi-trailing arms, coil springs and anti-roll bar
Brakes: vented discs front, drums rear
Tyres: 205/60 VR 15
Kerb weight: 940kg (2,070lb)

The interesting styling of this small two-seat convertible works well to produce a classic appearance

Volkswagen Corrado G60

Country of origin: Germany
Date: the 1991 specification should have the new narrow-angle 2.8-litre V6 178hp engine
Identity: a two-door 2 + 2 coupé
Engine: front-mounted transverse four-cylinder with alloy head and belt-driven ohc working four valves per cylinder; multi-point fuel injection; supercharged with intercooler; power 116kW (158PS) at 5,600rpm
Gears: five-speed manual; front-wheel drive
Capacity: 1,781cc
Bore and stroke: 81 × 86mm (3.19 × 3.38in)
Maximum speed: 210km/h (131mph); 0 to 97km/h (60mph) 8.7sec
Dimensions: wheelbase 2.47m (8ft 1.2in); length 4.05m (13ft 3.3in); width 1.67m (5ft 5.9in); height 1.32m (4ft 3.9in)
Chassis: front suspension independent Mac-Pherson struts and anti-roll bar; rear semi-independent torsion beam with trailing arms plus track-correcting mountings, coil springs and anti-roll bar
Brakes: vented discs front; solid discs rear; ABS optional
Tyres: 185/55 VR 15
Kerb weight: 1,155kg (2,544lb)

A rear spoiler moves up at speed – too low a speed in the UK (72km/h/ 45mph) and too high in Germany (120km/h/75mph)